Fortifying Pakistan
The Role of U.S. Internal
Security Assistance

Fortifying Pakistan

The Role of U.S. Internal Security Assistance

C. Christine Fair and Peter Chalk

UNITED STATES INSTITUTE OF PEACE PRESS
Washington, DC

Cover: photos by Christine Fair.

The views expressed in this book are those of the author alone. They do not necessarily reflect views of the United States Institute of Peace.

UNITED STATES INSTITUTE OF PEACE
1200 17th Street NW, Suite 200
Washington, DC 20036-3011

First published 2006

Printed in the United States of America

The paper used in this publication meets the minimum requirements of American National Standards for Information Science—Permanence of Paper for Printed Library Materials, ANSI Z39.48-1984.

Library of Congress Cataloging-in-Publication Data

Fair, C. Christine.
   Fortifying Pakistan : the role of U.S. internal security and law enforcement assistance / by C. Christine Fair and Peter Chalk.
      p. cm.
   Includes bibliographical references and index.
   ISBN-13: 978-1-929223-88-6 (softcover : alk. paper)
   ISBN-10: 1-929223-88-9 (softcover : alk. paper)
   1. Internal security—Pakistan. 2. Military assistance, American—Pakistan.
   3. United States—Foreign relations—Pakistan. 4. Pakistan—Foreign relations—
United States. I. Chalk, Peter. II. Title.
   HV8250.5.A3F67 2006
   355'.03254910973—dc22   2006011876

For Christine's husband, Jeffrey Kelley,
and Peter's wife and son, Tasha Enemark and Corinth Enemark-Chalk

Contents

Foreword by Ambassador Robert B. Oakley   ix

Preface   xiii

A Note on Terms of Reference, Methods, and Sources   xv

Glossary of Acronyms   xvii

Maps   xix

Introduction   1

1. Pakistan's Domestic Threat Environment   9

2. U.S. Assistance Programs to Pakistan   45

3. Assessment of U.S. Law Enforcement Assistance to Pakistan   61

Postscript   81

Notes   83

Bibliography   121

Index   143

About the Authors   163

Illustrations

Figures

1. Agency Administrative Structure in FATA   11

Tables

1. Deaths Resulting from Sunni-Shi'a Sectarian Violence, 2002–2004   27

2. Afghan Opium Statistics, 1994–2004   30

3. Opiate Seizures and Drug Arrests in Pakistan, 1996–2004   30

4. Most Corrupt Sectors in Pakistan according to Public Opinion   38

5. Average Bribe per Sector   39

6. U.S. Security Assistance and the Extant Pakistani Internal Threat Environment   63

Maps

1. Pakistan   xix

2. Districts of Pakistan's Northwest Frontier Province and FATA   xx

3. The Disputed Area of Jammu and Kashmir   xxi

Foreword

Over the past fifteen years a great deal has been learned about the critical importance of well-trained and -equipped police forces. They are indispensable in rebuilding failed states and preventing their collapse and in coping with powerful domestic and international organized armed criminal groups. Their responsibilities include helping to pacify various forms of terrorism and ethnic or sectarian militias and building durable police and judicial institutions for the rule of law. The United States Institute of Peace has been at the forefront in learning lessons about this process, applying them in practice, and understanding them in theory.

This volume by C. Christine Fair and Peter Chalk on Pakistan is the latest important contribution to the Institute's body of work. With a deep understanding of Pakistan's many security problems, the authors have undertaken a very impressive analysis based on years of painstaking research and make striking insights into how the problems might be addressed. They call the shots as they see them and tackle some highly difficult questions that do not lend themselves to easy answers.

The authors place the narrower issue of internal security reform and U.S. assistance in the broader context of Pakistan's external and internal security issues (e.g., relations with Kashmir and Afghanistan; global terrorism; and various Pakistan-based Islamic extremist groups such as Lashkar-e-Taiba, Jaish-e-Mohammad, the Taliban, and al-Qaeda). It is true that external and internal security issues cannot be separated. Nor can major progress be made in the reform of Pakistan's security forces without tackling the underlying problems caused by the activities and influence of these groups—some of which are threats to the Musharraf regime—on the internal security situation. Thus, the authors boldly call for closing down groups associated with the Kashmir resistance and those operating against Afghanistan out of Pakistani territory in the Federally Administered Tribal Areas (FATA) and Baluchistan as a prerequisite for fundamental reform of Pakistan's security and judicial sectors and for the ultimate success of U.S. assistance programs. A very tall order, this call raises questions about Pakistan's domestic and foreign political-religious-military dynamics and about the will, and even the ability, of the Musharraf regime to make a full-scale break with the extremist groups and to replace the opaque, ambivalent relationship that currently exists.

Moving from macro-security issues, the authors then take a more limited, practical look at U.S. civilian assistance to Pakistani security. As Pakistan is an ally in the global war on terrorism and Islamic extremism, the United States does not have the luxury of requiring a solution to the basic problems limiting the efficacy of Pakistan's security forces as a prerequisite for its assistance. Thus, the authors look at U.S. assistance in light of what it has achieved and what it can realistically be expected to achieve given the underlying problems. An important consideration—noted but not dealt with in detail—is the role of Pakistan's military forces and military intelligence, which has a very significant impact upon internal security and the various extremist groups and which receives large-scale U.S. assistance. In addition to the extremist groups considered in the first part of the book, the authors examine in some detail other major problems facing Pakistan's security forces, such as narcotics and broader smuggling, corruption, sectarian violence, and the educational environment, which encourages Islamic extremism rather than an acceptance of law and order.

In the face of these problems, the authors observe, U.S. civilian security assistance is directed toward four interrelated objectives:

- ❖ Bolstering counterterrorism capabilities
- ❖ Reinforcing instruments to confront criminal and other organizations that support extremism
- ❖ Addressing the underlying dearth of security and governance enabling extremism
- ❖ Helping the government to project its authority and the rule of law throughout Pakistan's national territory

In this context, the primary functions addressed by U.S. civilian assistance are counterterrorism, law enforcement, and counternarcotics. Geographically, the programs are focused primarily upon FATA and Baluchistan, both of which are infested by terrorism and narcotics trafficking involving Afghanistan, Iran, and Pakistan. The U.S. programs are administered by the Departments of State and Justice, the United States Agency for International Development, and the Drug Enforcement

Administration. The civilian programs in these regions are coordinated to the degree possible with Pakistan's military programs, which are assisted by the U.S. military and the Central Intelligence Agency. Key U.S. objectives in the border areas are to assist Pakistan's military and civilian forces in combating terrorism and narcotics (including through road building) and to assist in community development projects that promote greater acceptance of and cooperation with Pakistani security forces (including through school building). As the authors point out, the efficacy of Pakistani (and U.S.) programs in both FATA and Baluchistan is open to question, particularly given the strength of the opposition.

On a national level, the United States has chosen not to tackle the huge law enforcement problems caused by decades of poor education, training, and discipline and corruption among Pakistani police forces. U.S. training programs have been more narrowly focused on achievable tasks, but they have helped alleviate somewhat these basic problems and encouraged the government of Pakistan to undertake more comprehensive, long-term reform. Indeed, some niche U.S. programs on the national level have had very positive results. One of these is the Joint Working Group on Counterterrorism and Law Enforcement. It has not only enhanced the coordination of U.S. civilian security assistance but has also increased interagency cooperation among the several Pakistani internal security agencies.

Other useful programs are the Automated Fingerprint Identification System and the Personal Identification System. Both are computer-driven systems to identify persons entering and leaving the country or apprehended inside the country. Both have identified known and suspected terrorists—something that was previously more guesswork than science. Another successful U.S. innovation is the highly trained Counterterrorism Special Investigation Group, which is called upon by the government of Pakistan to investigate high-profile terrorist incidents (such as the attack on President Musharraf). Additional programs are still in the gestation phase.

In a concluding chapter, the authors review limitations on the reform of Pakistani internal security policies, programs, and practices. For example, they question the will at the top levels of government to deal with Islamist extremist groups and consider the problem of corruption within the bureaucracy. The authors also raise questions as to whether overall U.S. assistance to and policies toward Pakistan do enough to encourage development of a democratic system and civil society. These questions go well beyond issues of assistance to Pakistan's internal security.

The volume is a well-researched, highly informative analysis of Pakistan's internal security problems and U.S. assistance programs. It both raises basic questions of the highest policy significance and provides a good picture of what U.S. programs have been able to achieve. On balance, one concludes that there has been substantial progress despite the problems; that there is still a very long way to go; and that the U.S. investment in dollars, equipment, and effort is justified and worth continuing. Given the stakes involved, including those related to the stewardship of Pakistan's nuclear capabilities, the United States must continue to help Pakistan in its struggle against extremism.

Ambassador Robert B. Oakley
Washington, DC

Preface

The authors are first of all indebted to the numerous serving and retired officials, journalists, and analysts in both Pakistan and the United States who took the time to share their various insights and thoughts on the subject matter contained in this study.

A special debt of thanks is owed to Paul Stares, the director of the Center for Conflict Analysis and Prevention (formerly the Research and Studies Program) within the United States Institute of Peace, who supported this project from its inception and recognized its importance in the context of the global war on terrorism. The authors would additionally like to acknowledge a number of individuals who reviewed this draft and provided invaluable feedback on it, including Lt. Col. Kurt Meppen, a research fellow at the Institute; Stephen P. Cohen of the Brookings Institution; and Col. (ret.) John H. Gill. Additionally, the authors would like to express their gratitude to two individuals within the Institute's Center for Conflict Analysis and Prevention for their invaluable research and editorial support: Kerem Levitas, who is a program associate, and Isaac Congedo, who is a research assistant. Finally, the authors are grateful to Kurt Volkan, whose diligent editorial guidance did much to save them from their own prose. It goes without saying, however, that any omissions, errors, or deficiencies are the responsibility of the authors alone.

The intent of this study is to advance the interests of both the U.S. and Pakistan governments and to contribute to the development of a robust U.S.-Pakistan relationship. Equally, while aspects of this study are critical of both the United States and Pakistan, the authors trust the study will be recognized and understood as a good-faith effort to identify means to enhance the quality of life and governance of the people of Pakistan. The authors also hope that this study will be instrumental in stimulating further analysis and discussions of Pakistan's internal security reform.

A Note on Terms of Reference, Methods, and Sources

"Islamic" vs. "Islamist"

The popular press frequently conflates the terms "Islamic" with "Islamist." For example, it is not uncommon to read or hear the expression "Islamic terrorism" or "Islamic violence." This use is as unfortunate as it is erroneous. The term Islamist is an immediate derivation of Islamism, which is distinguished from the term Islamic by the fact that Islamic signifies religion and culture as it has developed over the last millennium of Islam's history. In contrast, Islamism is first and foremost a religiopolitical phenomenon with moorings in significant events of the twentieth century, such as the Iranian Revolution, the Soviet invasion of Afghanistan, and the Palestinian uprising against Israeli occupation. Thus, in this study, the terms Islamic and Islamist are not employed interchangeably. The term Islamic is used sparingly and only when specifically referencing cultural, religious, or artistic aspects of Islam. When describing religiopolitical phenomenon, the authors use the term Islamist. For example, it makes sense to use the expression "Islamic law" but not "Islamic militancy."[1]

Transliteration and Terms of Reference

This monograph discusses several militant groups that have been episodically proscribed only to emerge under new names, which are generally unfamiliar to most readers. For clarity, therefore, this study retains the original designations for these organizations. For example, although Lashkar-e-Taiba (LeT) now operates under the banner Jamaat ul Dawa, it is referred to throughout the study by the former name, as this is the most well-known and widely used name. Additionally, the study uses many Urdu and Perso-Arabic words that have different transliterations, most of which are equally acceptable. The authors have chosen to use spellings that are the closest to the Urdu pronunciation. Hence, "jihad" is chosen in preference of "jehad" and "Lashkar-e-Taiba" in preference of "Lashkar-e-Toiba." In instances where two alternative transliterations are available, the authors have adopted the simpler of the two. Thus, Jamaat Islami is used in lieu of Jama'at-e-Islami and other such variants.

Methods of Research and a Caveat on Sources

Given the sparse literature on Pakistan's internal security, much of the information contained in this study is of a primary nature obtained from interviews and discussions with officials, analysts, academics, researchers, and journalists in Pakistan, the United States, and, where relevant, India. Interview data always suffers from inherent limitations, such as selection bias and perspective bias, which may limit the generalizability of the respondents' observations. For example, the respondents' political positions, professional equities, and other forms of institutional vestedness may affect the data they provide. Respondents may even deliberately mislead or misinform to affect the authors' analyses.

This study also draws upon a thorough review of the open-source literature, including South Asian media sources. Unfortunately, journalism—while vibrant in the region—is not always accurate. The authors have made every effort to corroborate sources as much as possible and to exclude information that does not appear to be credible or reliable. The authors have also made every possible effort to ensure that this study reflects an objective assessment of the current state of Pakistan's internal security environment and of the utility of U.S. support to the country's law enforcement and civil justice community. Whether the authors have succeeded in doing so will be judged by the readers and by the robustness of their analyses. This study generally takes December 1, 2005, as its information cutoff point.

Glossary of Acronyms

AFIS	Automated Fingerprint Identification System
AIDS	Acquired Immunodeficiency Syndrome
ANF	Anti-Narcotics Task Force
ASS	Anjuman-e-Sipah-Sahaba
ATTA	Afghanistan Transit Trade Agreement
CIA	Central Intelligence Agency
CPI	Corruption Perception Index
CT	Counter Terrorism
DEA	Drug Enforcement Agency
DS/ATA	Diplomatic Security, Office of Antiterrorism Assistance
ESF	Economic Support Funds
FATA	Federally Administered Tribal Areas
FCR	Frontier Crime Regulation
FIA	Federal Investigative Agency
FIU	Financial Intelligence Unit
FMF	Foreign Military Financing
FMS	Foreign Military Sales
FOB	Forward Operating Base
GDP	Gross Domestic Product
GT	Grand Truck
GWOT	Global War on Terror
HIV	Human Deficiency Virus
HM	Hizbol Mujahadeen
HUJI	Harakat-ul-Jihad-e-Islami
HuM	Harkat-ul-Mujahadeen
IB	Intelligence Bureau
ICG	International Crisis Group
ICITAP	International Criminal Investigative Training Assistance Program
INL	Bureau of International Narcotics and Law Enforcement
IOM	International Organization for Migration
ISI	Inter-Services Intelligence
IV	Intravenous
J&K	Jammu and Kashmir
JeM	Jaish-e-Mohammad
JI	Jamaat Islami

JuA	Jamiat-ul-Ansar
JWG-CTLE	Joint Working Group on Counterterrorism and Law Enforcement
KESC	Karachi Electric Supply Corporation Limited
LeJ	Lashkar-e-Jhangvi
LeT	Lashkar-e-Taiba
MI	Ministry of the Interior
MMA	Muttahida Majlis-e-Amal
NAB	National Accountability Bureau
NACP	National AIDS Control Program
NCDB	National Criminal Database
NGO	nongovernmental organization
NOC	no-objection certificate
NWFP	North Western Frontier Province
OEF	Operation Enduring Freedom
PISCES	Personal Identification Security, Comparison and Evaluation System
PML	Pakistan Muslim League
PO	Police Order
PPP	Pakistan's People Party
S/CT	Office of Counterterrorism
SCBA	Supreme Court Bar Association
SIG	Special Investigation Group
SIU	Special Investigative Unit
SMP	Sipah-e-Muhammad Pakistan
SSG	Special Services Group
SSP	Sipah-e-Sahaba-Pakistan
SWAT	Special Weapons and Tactics
TI	Transparency International
TI-P	Transparency International-Pakistan
TJP	Tahrik-e-Jafaria
TNJF, TJF	Tehril-e-Nafaz Fiqh-e-Ja'fariyya
USAID	United States Agency for International Development
WAPDA	Pakistan Water and Development Authority
WMD	weapons of mass destruction

Pakistan

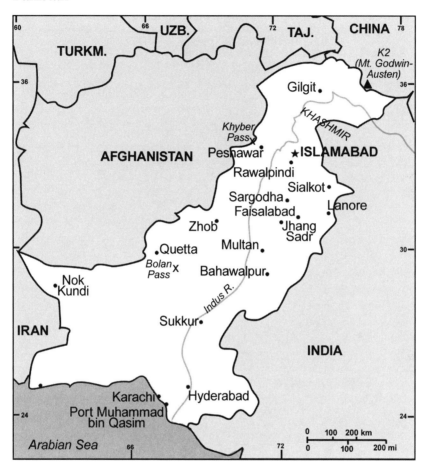

Courtesy of the University of Texas Libraries, University of Texas at Austin

Districts of Pakistan's Northwest Frontier Province and FATA

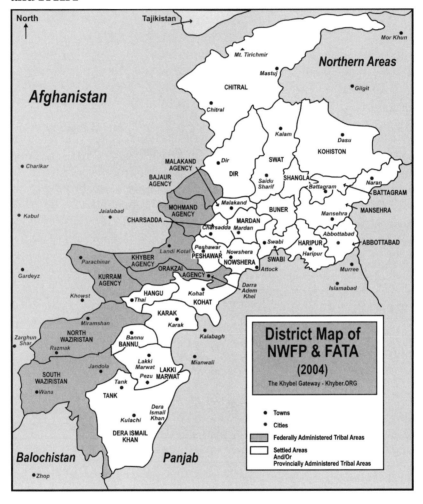

The Disputed Area of Jammu and Kashmir

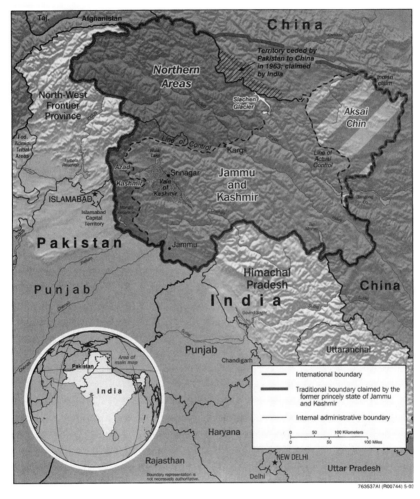

Courtesy of the University of Texas Libraries, University of Texas at Austin

Introduction

Background: Internal Security Matters

Within the South Asian region, Pakistan is today arguably one of the most important allied partners[1] of the United States. Since reversing its policy toward Afghanistan following the September 11 attacks, the country has emerged as a central partner in the Bush administration's global war on terror (GWOT),[2] playing a critical role in helping to degrade the operational capabilities of al-Qaeda and affiliated Taliban elements that fled Afghanistan in the wake of Operation Enduring Freedom (OEF).[3] Indeed, at the time of writing, Pakistan had rendered more suspected al-Qaeda operatives to the United States, including several high-profile commanders such as Khaled Sheikh Mohammad, Abu Farraj al-Libbi, and Ahmed Ghailani, than any other coalition partner.[4] Contrasting with these notable successes, however, is the reality that no high-level Taliban cadre has yet been captured.

Beyond the GWOT, the United States has numerous other salient interests in helping Pakistan fortify its internal security apparatus and counter sources of insecurity, such as those related to narcotics smuggling and abuse, money laundering, trafficking in persons, illegal migration, and the rendition of suspected terrorists. In addition, since the overt nuclearization of the South Asian subcontinent in 1998, one of the most enduring U.S. foreign policy goals has been to mitigate the possibility of an Indo-Pakistan war.

Several sources of tension exist between India and Pakistan, including territorial conflicts—the most significant of which is over Jammu and Kashmir—"extradition" disputes—particularly in relation to known or wanted criminals and others who Delhi considers to be terrorists—and security dilemmas arising from their nuclear and conventional arms race.[5] Dampening the destabilizing potential of these and other matters is widely recognized as vital both to securing and promoting security on the subcontinent and to limiting the potential operating space available to al-Qaeda, even if doing so will not in itself lead to total regional stability and security.

Although Pakistan is a state of central importance to ensuring the geostrategic stability of the wider South Asian region, it is afflicted by a multitude of domestic extremist and criminal threats and governance challenges. Terrorism, of many varieties, represents a particularly serious threat to the country; random killings and bomb attacks have occurred all too frequently over the past decade. Much of this recent violence has stemmed from rival Sunni and Shi'a sectarian groups,[6] while in the past it also came from antistatist militants fighting for a separate Mohajir province in Sindh. Additionally, ethnic tensions in Baluchistan and the activities of jihadists—including those allegedly backed by the army and Inter-Services Intelligence Directorate (ISI)—have emerged as serious threats to the state.[7]

Following Pakistan's decision to ally with the United States in the GWOT and to restrict the activities of Islamist militant groups operating within the country, several such groups began targeting President Pervez Musharraf, high-level members of his administration, and various foreign interests located in Pakistan. This development suggests that the security forces are not only losing much of their influence over some of their former and current proxies but, more troublingly, are also confronting an escalating "blow-back phenomenon" that they are increasingly unable to contain.[8]

While such a reorientation poses an obvious threat to the internal security of the Pakistani state, it also carries negative implications for U.S. and international efforts to stabilize Afghanistan and is serving to further complicate Islamabad's historically problematic relations with India. Moreover, the investigation into the July 2005 London Underground bombings has revealed that several individuals who were either responsible for the attacks or in some way tied to them may have sought militant training in Pakistan. Accordingly, Pakistan's domestic situation has direct relevance to the international community as well.[9]

Further complicating Pakistan's internal security situation is an entrenched and substantial milieu of organized criminal activity. Syndicates exist in many cities, engaging in everything from documentation forgery and money laundering to licit and illicit goods smuggling and human trafficking. Just as significantly, what effectively amounts to institutionalized graft has had a deleterious effect on Islamabad's governing legitimacy and effectiveness—the country is consistently ranked in the upper ten percent of Transparency International's (TI) Corruption Perception Index (CPI).[10] Although the United States is not directly affected by these various manifestations of organized crime, they do represent a subset of the transnational problems that the Bush administration has identified as a growing threat to U.S. national security and international stability. Moreover, they pose a direct challenge to the domestic stability of a state that is of considerable geostrategic significance to Washington.

Unfortunately, Pakistan has only a limited capacity to deal with these myriad threats. The state has no centralized criminal database and only rudimentary forensic capabilities. Further, Pakistan's police lack resources and basic investigative tools and are generally unschooled in how to secure a crime scene and follow custodial procedures for collected evidence. As a consequence, there are few technical and human means available within Pakistan for collecting and assembling evidence against criminal or terrorist suspects.[11] The immigration systems at Pakistan's ports of arrival are equally archaic. With the introduction of U.S. computerized systems at the country's major international airports, Pakistan has only recently begun to operationalize a digitized system for tracking those entering and leaving the country. Land borders suffer from even greater deficiencies, particularly those in the remote northern areas where frontier posts are largely devoid of any formal regulations or controls.[12] It should be noted, however, that Pakistan is not unique in these regards: most states in South Asia suffer similar deficiencies.[13]

Besides an inadequate police and immigration structure, Pakistan is also in dire need of judicial reform. Not only are federal and local officials subject to coercion and manipulation by political authorities, elites, and crime syndicates, few in the country understand their rights much less avail themselves of appropriate accountability, review, and appeal mechanisms.[14] Just as seriously, corruption and highly inefficient trial and conviction processes have served to dramatically undermine public confidence in the justice system; many simply turn to extralegal remedies for redress.[15]

Faced with these collective challenges, Islamabad has made certain nascent attempts to address them. For example, Pakistan has taken steps to modernize its outdated nineteenth-century police ordinance. Additionally, in 2002, Pakistan and the United States launched several initiatives to help strengthen the state's law enforcement capacity; this includes the formation of a Joint Working Group on Counter Terrorism and Law Enforcement (JWG-CTLE). As discussed in chapter 2, the JWG-CTLE met for the first time in May 2003 and is emerging as a key conduit for addressing a wide array of mutual U.S.-Pakistani security concerns.

While the JWG-CTLE has made a promising start—if only by high-lighting just how underresourced Pakistan's counterterrorism and law enforcement mechanisms remain—a robust and concerted commitment to further internal security reform is still needed on the part of Pakistan. To ensure that such reform proceeds as effectively and smoothly as possible, sustained and attentive involvement from the United States and other international partners, such as Great Britain and Japan, will be required. Pakistan will also need to permanently close down those groups that claim to be fighting for the liberation of the portion of Kashmir under Indian control,[16] but currently there is little indication the government is moving to do so. This is at least in part because of apprehensions within Pakistan about India's intentions vis-à-vis the disputed province and the persistent belief that Delhi seeks to sideline Islamabad from any resolution related to the embattled region.[17] Until there is a final settlement to this protracted territorial conflict, Pakistan will not be willing to strategically abandon the use of jihadist organizations; Islamabad does not see any other means of persuading its larger and stronger neighbor to come to the negotiating table in good faith.

Indeed, despite the generally positive atmospherics of the ongoing Indo-Pakistan dialogue, Indian sources complain that Pakistan is unwilling to render known criminal and terrorist fugitives to India[18] and announced in August 2005 that militant Islamist infiltration is again on the rise, a charge vigorously disputed by Musharraf.[19] However, U.S. officials inter-viewed in Islamabad shared this belief that infiltration was increasing.[20] Unfortunately, Pakistan's dogged pursuit of militancy as a tool of its foreign policy will continue to have repercussions for the domestic integrity of the state—particularly as uncontrolled jihadist groups increasingly begin to see the government as their enemy—and continue to limit political and economic opportunities for its citizens.

As noted, Washington has an active interest in ensuring the continued strengthening of Pakistan's internal security. Viable law enforcement, immigration, and judicial structures are needed for shoring up the coun-try's domestic stability and should help militate against the (very remote) possibility of a collapsed nuclear-armed state.[21] A stable Pakistan would also diminish the opportunities for nonstate actors to acquire fissile material or nuclear technology. In addition, fortifying Pakistan against internal threats may foster an environment that is conducive to establishing successful confidence-building measures throughout the subcontinent.

However, while improved internal security programs within Pakistan are a necessary—albeit insufficient—part of ensuring regional stability, the authors recognize that the effectiveness of these programs will ultimately hinge upon whether Pakistan has the political will and sustained intent to make these programs work. One of the key challenges for the United States in defining its future policy toward Pakistan, therefore, is to determine how best to support current advocates of law enforcement reform in Pakistan. Clearly, Washington cannot be expected to fund all of the country's needed law enforcement reform programs. Rather, Washington should take a measured approach by identifying critical internal security areas within Pakistan and developing programs that address those areas, prioritizing according to likely benefit, time horizon of benefit, likelihood of long-term untoward consequences, financial cost, and opportunity costs to other potential programs.[22]

In addition, the United States must map out a comprehensive, long-term strategy for assisting the development of Pakistan's internal security and for guiding future investments in counterterrorist and crime-fighting initiatives within the country. Because the impacts of such programs are long term, this will require Washington to pursue a dedicated and sustained relationship with Islamabad that can endure the vicissitudes of political exigencies.[23] The United States must also continue to pressure Pakistan to ensure that it does not retrench from the advances it has made thus far in countering Islamist militancy and its supporting structures.

Objectives and Scope of the Study

This study offers a comprehensive examination of Pakistan's internal security environment and the effectiveness of its criminal justice structures and assesses the impact and utility of principal U.S. initiatives that have been enacted to help Pakistan fortify its internal security arrangements. The authors specifically intend to (1) identify the strengths and weaknesses of America's various support efforts; (2) highlight those areas that require more dedicated resources; and (3) delineate specific weaknesses emanating from both the U.S. and Pakistan governments that limit the efficacy of the current assistance programs.

As this study is focused only on internal security (sometimes referred to as "civilian security") programs and efforts to build capacity in the civilian sector, programs executed by the U.S. Department of Defense and/or conducted through Pakistan's Ministry of Defense are outside its purview. For example, Coalition Support Funds (CSF) are not discussed. Even though payments from these funds comprise an important source of hard currency for Pakistan ($1.32 billion between January 2003 and September 2004), they are made by the Defense Department to Pakistan's Ministry of Defense and therefore do not directly target civilian capabilities. Further, their primary aim is to reimburse Pakistan for the resources it has deployed in support of U.S. operations in Afghanistan.[24]

The authors believed that taking on this study was important for several reasons. First, Pakistan is the recipient of considerable and diverse U.S. resources. Given the scope of this investment, it makes sense to assess the utility of these expenditures. Second, because Pakistan must have both the will and the capability to counter the various threats it faces and because the United States has several specific security interests with respect to Pakistan, it is necessary to examine whether Islamabad is receiving the type of assistance that it needs for its own requirements and whether this suite of programs best serves U.S. interests and objectives. Third, Pakistan is an enormously important partner in the GWOT and the concomitant struggle against violent extremism. It is therefore important that its government remains a fully cooperative and allied partner in the near and policy-relevant future. It is equally critical that Pakistan develops into a fully stable and functioning democracy that is able to live at peace with itself and its neighbors over the long term. Determining how U.S. security assistance affects Pakistan's long-term development is, therefore, a valid area of research. Indeed, short-term initiatives may adversely affect longer-term goals. This issue will be discussed throughout the study.

Organization and Expected Benefits of the Study

Chapter 1 discusses the array of domestic security challenges confronting Pakistan and the specific ways in which they negatively affect the country's stability. Chapter 2 looks at current U.S.-funded efforts to enhance

Islamabad's domestic criminal justice and security environments and examines relevant programs both in terms of their stated objectives and resource allocation. Chapter 3 considers the relevance of U.S. law enforcement assistance to Pakistan, equating the prioritization of individual initiatives—as determined by Washington—to the seriousness of extant security challenges within the country—as determined by Islamabad. It concludes with a number of policy prescriptions that can be followed to better design initiatives for strengthening the viability and robustness of Pakistan's security and judicial machinery. This, in turn, will benefit wider U.S. geostrategic objectives in South Asia.

The authors believe this study makes two significant contributions to the current understanding of the evolving security relationship between the United States and Pakistan. First, it provides a comprehensive overview of Pakistan's internal security considerations, both in the context of threat assessments and policy responses. To date, this type of integrated analysis has not featured prominently in much of the contemporary research on Pakistan. At a time when Islamabad's domestic viability is increasingly being linked both to the GWOT and to general stability in the South Asian region, addressing this lacuna is emerging as an increasingly important priority.

Second, the study links the future course of the Musharraf government's internal security policy to broader U.S. strategic imperatives—another issue that has yet to be comprehensively dealt with in the relatively sparse literature on this subject.[25] Ensuring that Pakistan remains stable and fully in control of its territory is of crucial importance to the Bush administration, particularly in terms of helping to consolidate post-Taliban reconstruction in Afghanistan, maintaining the nuclear geostrategic balance on the Indian subcontinent, and stemming ongoing Islamist extremist activity throughout South Asia (much of which has been directly tied to wider, pan-Islamist imperatives). Determining how Pakistan's evolving domestic setting will affect Washington's ability to pursue its interests in this part of the world, therefore, is an important topic worthy of examination and discussion.

Pakistan's Domestic Threat Environment

P akistan is confronting a mosaic of threats to its internal stability. Perhaps understandably, U.S. and Western security officials are concerned principally with the growing groundswell of jihadist terrorism that has emerged in the country and that is now adversely affecting a key ally in the wider GWOT. Although jihadist terrorism is undoubtedly a central concern, the array of challenges confronting the Musharraf regime extend well beyond this and include sectarian extremism, drug trafficking, illegal commodity smuggling, endemic corruption, and systemic problems with the provision of justice and law enforcement.[1] Each of these challenges is discussed below not only in terms of their scope, dimensions, and causal factors but also in terms of the risk they pose to Pakistan's internal security.

Jihadist Terrorism

Scope, Dimensions, and Causal Factors

Law enforcement and intelligence personnel within Pakistan generally agree that jihadist terrorism currently constitutes the country's number one security challenge.[2] Most Pakistani commentators and some external observers assert that this particular threat either stems from or has been exacerbated by the U.S.-led GWOT and Musharraf's support for it. Since 9/11, Pakistan's national policymaking on the terrorism front has been galvanized and framed by four specific interrelated concerns: (1) foreign jihadist activities in the semiautonomous Federally Administered Tribal Areas (FATA)[3]; (2) the observed reorientation of several prominent militant groups operating in Kashmir; (3) the influence of Pakistan's educational institutions; and (4) the involvement of security forces in violence.

Foreign Jihadist Activities in FATA

Since the onset of Operation Enduring Freedom (OEF) in October 2001, considerable attention has been focused on FATA, where many militants are thought to have relocated from Afghanistan. Internal control in this region follows a colonial-era system that relies upon representatives of the federal administration (political agents) working in concert with tribal leaders *(maliks)*. To understand the importance of FATA in garnering and fostering a strong extremist jihadist presence in Pakistan, a detailed discussion of extant governing arrangements in the area is first needed.

With the departure of the British from the Indian subcontinent in 1947, the tribal areas were no longer bound by the various treaties forged by colonial administrators.[4] Constitutionally, the onus for securing new governance arrangements in FATA lay with the nascent state of Pakistan, which quickly extracted an agreement from the *maliks*. In exchange for greater autonomy and control of the tribal areas, the *maliks* would recognize FATA as an integral component of Pakistan; would provide support and assistance to the state as and when necessary; and would maintain friendly relations with the people of the settled districts. Additional accords in 1951 and 1952 devolved further authority to the tribal areas.[5]

Since Pakistan's launch of military operations in FATA in the spring of 2004, Pakistani and foreign observers have frequently commented that the tribal areas have traditionally remained beyond the official purview of the government.[6] However, these axiomatic constructs of FATA as a "no-go zone" or an "ungoverned space" are not strictly speaking correct. First, FATA is constitutionally subject to the executive authority of the state. Second, the president is authorized to give directions to the provincial governor of the Northwest Frontier Province (NWFP) relating to the administration of any part of the tribal areas and to delegate the responsibility for ensuring the proper application of Pakistan's federal laws should they be enacted in the region. Finally, the constitution specifically gives the president the right to set regulations for the "peace and good government of [the] Federally Administered Tribal Areas or any part thereof."[7]

The political agents have primary responsibility for administering the agencies within FATA. These individuals constitute both the primary source of local authority and the key conduit through which the functions of the state are coordinated. They rely upon their structured relations with the *maliks*—and, to a great extent, their personal influence with them—to ensure the cooperation of the tribesmen and to promulgate state policy through a unique system of tribal and territorial responsibility. Notably, a political agent is accountable only to the NWFP provincial governor, who, in turn, serves as the president's official representative in the tribal areas.[8]

The political agents are able to draw on a number of supplementary personnel to execute policy and manage tribal affairs, including *naib* (assistant) political agents, *tehsildars*, and *naib tehsildars*.[9] The political agents also have certain quasi-police forces at their disposal, such as the Khasadars. Figure 1 illustrates some of these arrangements and relations. Further, the political agents and *maliks* work together to institute policy through the use of tribal mechanisms, such as the *jirga*. The *jirga* is a consultative mechanism that gathers village leadership to deliberate on issues and to disseminate collective decisions throughout the tribal system. The *jirga* can form tribal *lashkars* (militias) to enforce *jirga* outcomes if needed.

In addition to the Khasadars and the *jirga*'s tribal *lashkars*, several paramilitary organizations provide internal control and security within FATA, including two separate organizations known by the same initials.[10] The Frontier Corps (FC), which is manned by military officers, maintains a presence in the tribal agencies between the Durand Line and the outer limits of the settled areas; and the Frontier Constabulary (FC), which is staffed by police officers, is employed in the regions defined by the limits of the tribal agencies and the settled districts.[11]

Figure 1. Agency Administrative Structure in FATA

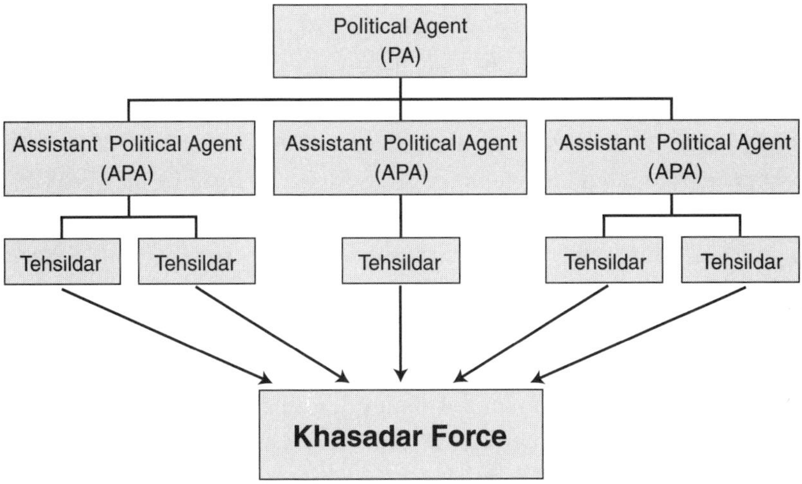

The political agents manage law and order within FATA through a con-
troversial colonial-era legal framework known as the Frontier Crime Regulation (FCR). One of the principal tenets of this structure is the notion of
collective responsibility. That is, fellow tribe members of suspected criminal perpetrators can be punished—even if they had no involvement with
the alleged infraction—provided that "solid supporting information" is
available to the authorities. Once a political agent—or assistant political
agent—passes judgment, there is very limited recourse for appeal. This
structure has been labeled draconian and has drawn the ire of human rights
activists who decry that political agents have all-encompassing authority in
such cases and that innocent persons may be wrongly punished.[12]

Several factors have been especially significant in facilitating the penetration of foreign jihadists into FATA. For example, most residents of
FATA and the tribal areas are Pakhtun and as such follow *pakhtunwali*, the
honor code of the Pakhtuns.[13] *Pakhtunwali* purportedly stresses, among
other things, *melmastia* (unconditional hospitality), which must be
extended to both coreligionists, whether Pakhtuns or non-Pakhtuns, and
even members of other religious communities. During fieldwork on this
issue, one of this study's authors learned from scholars at the University of
Peshawar that Afghan Sikhs have sought and received shelter from Pakhtuns in FATA.[14]

Melmastia, therefore, may help explain why FATA has provided a geographic space that has been open and receptive to the influx of foreign
Islamists. For instance, after the Soviet Union's withdrawal from Afghanistan, many of these battle-hardened militants—denied return by their
countries of origin—stayed on in FATA where they were welcomed as
jihadi heroes and allowed to marry local women. These are the persons
whom Pakistanis tend to refer to as "Arab Afghans." It should be noted that
intermarriages between foreign (i.e., non-Pakhtun) fighters and Pakhtun
women are themselves *major* violations of another tenet of *pakhtunwali*,
which vigorously discourages marriages (*wadah*) to non-Pakhtuns and thus
attests to the somewhat adaptable nature of *pakhtunwali*.[15] Contrary to
popular belief, however, this notion of hospitality is not strictly speaking
unconditional. For example, if a family housing an individual is under
threat for providing such protection and if there are other housing options
available, the guest is obliged to leave. Similarly, families will not continue

to house a guest if their honor is violated, such as through inappropriate behavior by the guest.[16]

While these complex communal and social structures played a central role in shaping the relocation calculus of Taliban and al-Qaeda fugitives, especially following the U.S. operations against Tora Bora in late 2001, *pakhtunwali* and *melmastia* alone cannot account for the penetration of foreign jihadists into the FATA. Equally as important was the fact that the Pakistani government used this territory—because of its proximity to the theatre of conflict—as one of several staging areas in the struggle to oust the Soviets from Afghanistan.[17] Further, the fundamental transformation of historical tribal power structures within FATA has enabled a robust presence of foreign fighters there. This realignment of power centers has come about as a result of some thirty years of incessant warfare and the nearly concurrent introduction of Wahabbist ideologies during the 1980s.[18] Specifically, prior to the anti-Soviet conflict in Afghanistan, the mullahs were minor actors when compared to the *maliks* and the political agents, who were then the primary power brokers in a given agency. But this no longer appears to be the case; today the mullahs reportedly enjoy influence and authority that had been hitherto unknown to them.

While the exact nature of the contemporary tribal power structure in FATA needs further study, at least one former high-ranking ISI official explained that even the Pakistan Army has had an inaccurate understanding of the contemporary mullah-*malik* relationship and how it has changed. This official believed that the army's "intelligence gap" on this issue was one of the reasons for the army's numerous difficulties in 2004, when it intervened in FATA for the first time, launching military operations in South Waziristan. (The Pakistan Army is currently conducting military operations in North Waziristan.)[19] By the time the operations ended in December 2004, the army had killed 302 militants and detained 656 of them. Some 80 percent of these militants were foreign, mostly comprised of Afghan Arabs, Uzbeks, and Chechens, with a small number of Uighurs from China. Pakistani and non-Pakistani officials alike point to these figures as concrete evidence that external Islamist fighters have penetrated FATA.[20] Indeed, Washington has repeatedly portrayed FATA as the locus of a new logistical and operational beachhead for transnational jihadist extremism.

However, what has not been often mentioned by observers of Pakistan's ongoing military operations in FATA is that only a fraction of these foreign fighters are believed to have arrived in FATA after the onset of OEF. As Pakistani intelligence analysts maintain, many of these persons were in the area long before 9/11. Moreover, these analysts also claim that many of these "terrorists" were actually wanted criminals who had sought shelter in FATA from Pakistani authorities and that Pakistan has been using these operations as cover to pursue individuals wanted within the country for reasons that have nothing to do with the GWOT.[21]

Even if fewer foreign fighters fled to FATA than previously believed, the situation there remains highly relevant to the prosecution of the GWOT. The 2004 capture of Abu Farraj al-Libbi, a close confidant of Osama Bin Laden who is believed to have coordinated various assassination attempts against Musharraf (see below), testifies to this fact. Although he was arrested in the Northwest Frontier town of Mardan, al-Libbi was one of the Arab Afghans who made FATA their home following the Soviet pullout from Afghanistan. Prior to his arrest, al-Libbi had lived in Waziristan for eighteen years. Married to a local Pakistani, he learned Pashto and Urdu fluently and was fully integrated into the communal structure of the tribal areas.[22]

Although al-Libbi is now in U.S. custody, the Central Intelligence Agency (CIA) believes that the tribal areas continue to be an important home for the residual Bin Laden network—serving, allegedly, as the base for an "elite" unit dedicated to preparing for and coordinating major anti-Western attacks. The CIA contends that this cell, which is dispersed but able to communicate with regional affiliates around the world, now acts as the central operational hub of al-Qaeda and is presently in the process of finalizing plans for another spectacular terrorist attack.[23] Although Pakistani security sources reject these specific assertions, arguing that the 2004 offensives in South Waziristan—which were allegedly undertaken with the explicit support of local Pakhtun elders—have decisively eroded any foreign jihadist presence in FATA, they do concede that some Waziris probably continue to give succor to al-Qaeda affiliates, not only because of misplaced religious loyalties but also because of lucrative monetary incentives. For this and other reasons, the U.S. and Pakistani intelligence communities generally concur that the region needs to remain a focus of ongoing counterterrorism efforts.[24]

Officials in Islamabad note that while FATA may still be used as a con-duit to cross into Pakistani territory and should be a concern, the densely populated urban districts of Baluchistan, Punjab, and Sindh also pose numerous security challenges. Representatives from Pakistan's Federal Investigative Agency (FIA) and Ministry of the Interior (MoI) argue that the heightened U.S.-supported military presence along the northwestern border has forced foreign jihadists to seek refuge in cities such as Quetta, Faisalabad, Lahore, Rawalpindi, and Karachi—all of which provide a viable transportation and communication infrastructure for logistical and opera-tional planning. Law enforcement is ineffective in these cities and, in the case of Karachi, there is a large settled Arab population into which foreign-ers can disappear. Of significant note, some of al-Qaeda's more "high-value" assets are known to have operated in these cities and four of the group's most senior operational planners have been captured in these urban areas: Abu Zubaydah (caught in Faisalabad); Khaled Sheik Moham-mad (caught in Rawalpindi); and Ramzi Binalshib and Sheikh Ahmed Salim (both caught in Karachi).[25]

The Reorientation of Prominent Deobandi Kashmir-Focused Groups

Jihadist *tanzeems* (militant outfits) operating in Kashmir have historically fallen into two categories: those that are comprised of primarily Kashmiri cadres, such as al Badr and Hizbol Mujahadeen (HM); and those that are predominantly non-Kashmiri in composition, such as the Ahle-e-Hadith *tanzeem* Lashkar-e-Taiba (LeT) and prominent Deobandi groups,[26] which includes Jaish-e-Mohammad (JeM), Harkat-ul-Mujahadeen (HuM), and Harakat-ul-Jihad-e-Islami (HUJI).[27] Many of these groups, such as LeT, al Badr, and HM, have retained their focus upon Indian-administered Kash-mir and the Indian hinterland. However, as a result of shifts in Pakistan's policies starting in late 2001, several of the Deobandi jihadist *tanzeems*[28]—most notably JeM, HuM, and HUJI—have begun to target Musharraf and other elements of the Pakistani state.[29] This recent reorientation of promi-nent jihadist *tanzeems* is a very serious threat to Islamabad.

Pakistan's decision to ally with the United States in the GWOT was one of the first factors that initiated a change in the Deobandi organizations' operational focus. JeM was one of the first groups to bridle at this relation-ship. In fact, certain elements within JeM wanted to attack U.S. interests in

Pakistan after the launch of OEF, but JeM's then-leader Masood Azhar favored compliance with Pakistan's new policy direction as a political expediency. Other group leaders, such as Maulana Abdul Jabbar (alias Umar Farooq), disagreed with Azhar and took over the organization. Whereas Azhar is believed to be in protective custody for staying in step with Islamabad, Jabbar now leads the proscribed JeM splinter group, Jamaat-ul-Furqaan, which has actively targeted Pakistan's government.[30]

A second prominent catalyst of JeM's reorientation is what Pakistan-based analysts describe as Islamabad's "moderated-jihad" strategy—that is, the government's attempts to calibrate the jihad by placing limits on militant activities in Jammu and Kashmir (J&K) and the Indian hinterland.[31] According to these analysts, this new approach permits Islamabad to continue the peace process with Delhi while simultaneously maintaining the option of resuming and increasing militant activities should negotiations collapse or fail to produce tangible results. By keeping militant activities at a historically low level, this moderated-jihad strategy has resulted in substantially less international censure toward Pakistan for its continuing support of jihadist elements.

Pakistan has been motivated to pursue this moderated-jihad strategy both for external and internal reasons. Islamabad's policy of proxy warfare came under renewed international scrutiny following the JeM- (and possibly LeT-) backed assault on the Indian Parliament (Lok Sabha) in December 2001 and the ensuing yearlong military standoff between Indian and Pakistan. International pressure on Pakistan then peaked following the LeT-prosecuted massacre of military wives and children at Kaluchak in Indian-administered Kashmir on May 14, 2002. India, which had been mobilizing its forces since December 2001, considered punitive military strikes in retaliation. This "crisis within a crisis" prompted swift and decisive U.S. action. In June 2002, Deputy Secretary of State Richard Armitage went to Islamabad to extract Pakistan's promise to abandon its reliance upon militants and to cease the infiltration of militants into Indian-administered Kashmir.[32] This military standoff, with the specter of nuclear exchange looming over it, galvanized vigorous international pressure upon both Pakistan and India to reconcile the Kashmiri impasse.[33]

Apart from this external pressure to reoptimize its Kashmir strategy, Pakistan has recognized the threat these militant groups pose to its own internal security and has been properly motivated to rethink its Kashmir strategy.[34] This recognition is manifested, for example, in Musharraf's calls for "enlightened moderation."[35] While groups such as al Badr and HM remain under the effective control of Pakistani intelligence—and, hence, can be influenced to follow the moderated-jihad strategy—some U.S. and Pakistani analysts believe that the splintering of JeM was an object lesson to Islamabad and demonstrated that the intelligence agency no longer had complete control over some of its erstwhile proxies. Indeed, over the past four years, militants within JeM have systematically redirected the focus of their aggression toward the Pakistani state, while HuJI and various splinters of HuM have also taken on an explicit anti-Pakistani line.[36] For example, both JeM and HuJI, along with renegade military personnel—mainly junior and noncommissioned officers and enlisted cadres—have been implicated in high-level assassination attempts on President Musharraf, Prime Minister Shaukat Aziz, and Lt. Gen. Ahsan Saleem Hayat, the Karachi Corps commander.[37]

According to some U.S. analysts, "globalized" elements within LeT may also have begun participating in operations beyond Indian-administered Kashmir and India proper. Such persons base this claim partly upon recent Pakistani reports on LeT's Web-based materials and the group's annual three-day *ijtimah* (convention), during which speakers made various proclamations that were described as virulently anti-Western in tone.[38] However, longtime Pakistani analysts of LeT argue that these U.S. analysts lack a historical appreciation of the organization and that such claims are more a reflection of the U.S. analysts' own limited understanding of the organization than a reflection of any reorientation of LeT's activities. They reject the notion that LeT is globalizing, noting that LeT is one of the more ideologically unified and disciplined groups to have fought in Kashmir and that it is, therefore, not prone to the type of anti-Pakistani splintering that has befallen HuM, HuJI, and JeM. They also note that despite its long-standing claim to be international in focus, LeT has largely restricted its operations to Indian-administered Kashmir and India.[39]

Regardless, LeT does not have to be global in focus to be of great consequence to the region and beyond. For example, LeT was behind the attack on India's Red Fort in December 2000 and the Kaluchak massacre in May 2002, and it may have been involved in the strike against the Indian

Parliament in December 2001.[40] The two latter attacks nearly precipitated all-out war between India and Pakistan. The potential to initiate such conflict, with the attendant risk of nuclear escalation, underscores the menace to regional security posed by LeT and like-minded groups. Further, Abu Zubaydah, a senior al-Qaeda operator, was arrested in 2002 in a LeT safe house in Faisalabad. This strongly suggests that members of the group have actively cooperated with al-Qaeda and possibly assisted with the movement of its cadres throughout Pakistan.[41] There have also been periodic allegations that LeT has been instrumental in recruiting Islamists to engage U.S. forces in Iraq. However, U.S. officials interviewed for this study cannot confirm this assertion and indeed cast serious doubts upon the veracity of these and related claims.[42]

Concerns about LeT and JeM also surfaced with the July 2005 attacks on the London Underground; at least one of the perpetrators was alleged to have visited LeT headquarters in Muridke and made contact with JeM activists involved in the 2002 assault on an Islamabad church.[43] Despite the popular belief that these individuals received military training in Pakistan, at the time of writing, none of the more grandiose claims has been substantiated. Further, analysts strongly doubt that under the current circumstances groups such as LeT would permit a foreigner to participate in such activities.[44]

The Radicalizing Influences of Pakistan's Educational Institutions

Pakistan's various educational institutions and the instruction they impart have also contributed to Pakistan's problems with jihadist violence. In recent years, Pakistan's *madaris* (plural of *madrassah*) have garnered intense scrutiny and stand accused of indoctrinating Pakistan's youth and fostering among the polity a sentiment that is sympathetic to militant jihad. Unfortunately, there are no reliable sources for the number of *madaris* within Pakistan and the percentage of Pakistan's students who attend them. For example, Jessica Stern has claimed, without verifiable evidence, that there are 40,000 to 50,000 *madaris* within Pakistan.[45] Peter Singer similarly suggests that there could be as many as 45,000 in the country.[46] In contrast, the ISI claims that there are roughly 11,000 in Pakistan,[47] of which 5,800 are not registered with the Ministry of Education.[48]

Madrassah enrollment figures are similarly problematic. The popular press in Pakistan and elsewhere has suggested that anywhere from 500,000 to 1.5 million students attend *madaris* in any given year, while the International Crisis Group (ICG) estimates that from 1 to 1.7 million children are enrolled in Pakistani *madaris*.[49] Regrettably, these reports do not principally rely on verifiable data sources; rather, they nearly exclusively employ interview data and do not take into account other forms of data that could lead to more precise figures. To help address this empirical lacuna, a 2005 research team comprised of persons from the World Bank and Harvard University's Kennedy School of Government undertook the first and only empirically grounded assessment of Pakistan's full-time *madrassah* enrollment figures. This team found that perhaps fewer than 1 percent of enrolled students actually attends *madaris* full-time in Pakistan (159,225 students were enrolled in *madaris* out of a total of 22 million enrolled students).[50]

While the exact number of *madaris* and the number of students they claim are unknown, what is known is that virtually all of these institutions emphasize instruction that is wholly religious and sectarian in nature and is aimed toward producing religious teachers and scholars. Many are thought to host outside demagogues that espouse virulently anti-Western, anti-American, and anti-Indian doctrines, although empirical evidence on the extent of this practice is lacking. Several *madaris* are directly linked to the ideological teachings of proscribed groups operating in Pakistan, including LeT, JeM, and the Sunni sectarian group, the Anjuman-e-Sipah-Sahaba (ASS), subsequently renamed Sipah-e-Sahaba Pakistan (SSP).[51]

Besides providing religious—and possibly Islamist—indoctrination, certain *madaris* are also thought to play a direct role in propagating sectarian and jihadist extremism. Some analysts speculate that some schools funded from persons and organizations based in the Middle East provide a measure of military training—both to Pakistani and foreign students—under the veneer of spiritual guidance and instruction.[52] One 2003 World Bank study estimates that as many as 15 to 20 percent of Pakistan's *madaris* may provide this type of "extracurricular" activity,[53] although other studies put the estimate closer to 10 percent.[54] In addition, various facilities may act as a "sieve" for identifying, narrowing, and selecting suitable candidates for concerted terrorist training in designated Islamist *tanzeem* camps.[55]

Despite its historical support for Islamist militancy—especially in the context of the Kashmir theater—Pakistan has become increasingly concerned about the activities of *madaris*, especially in the wake of the 2003 assassination attempts on President Musharraf. Even before 2001, Pakistan initiated various campaigns to reform *madaris*, although none bore fruit. In January 2005, numerous Pakistani officials described to the authors Pakistan's then-current policy toward *madaris*. All schools were required to (1) mix religious subjects with secular studies (such as mathematics and science); (2) publicize the source of their funding; and (3) refuse entry to any international student that does not have a no-objection certificate (NOC) issued from his or her home country that validates his or her security bona fides.[56]

This policy, like its predecessors, was short-lived. In September 2005, the government announced yet another *madrassah* reform program following talks with the representatives of the Ittehad-e-Tanzeem ul-Madaris-e-Deeni (ITMD), an umbrella organization for five Islamic seminary associations that claims to control the vast majority (13,000) of *madaris* in Pakistan. (The reader is correct to be dismayed by the dizzying array of numbers bandied about. Unfortunately, there is simply no authoritative source on this issue.) Under this new deal, the ITMD agreed to register some 9,000 *madaris* provided that the government jettisoned the requirement that the *madaris* report sources of funding and made concessions related to foreign students attending them.[57]

While the vast majority of Pakistan's students—70 percent according to the 2005 World Bank and Kennedy School study—attend the country's public schools,[58] the national public school curriculum is accused of teaching the supreme value of militant jihad. Notwithstanding this accusation, the national curriculum promulgates versions of history that demonize non-Muslims and aggrandize the contributions of Islam to the region, distorts India's role in the subcontinent, and inculcates children with a distinctly sectarian outlook.[59] Husain Haqqani, a former senior Pakistani official and journalist who has pursued an academic career in the United States, has marshaled evidence that these curricular elements were introduced under Ayub Khan in the 1950s. According to his widely received analysis, Pakistan understood that early insertion of these ideological teachings into the national curriculum would do much to create future generations of youth who could be recruited to become *mujahadeen*.[60] While there have been various public statements about the necessity for curricular reform, there have been no substantive advances thus far. Over the last year, for instance, national curricular reform has sparked fierce debate over the proper place of jihad in Pakistan's biology curriculum, although no one appears to be asking publicly why jihad *belongs* in the national biology curriculum in the first place.[61]

Involvement of Security Forces in Islamist Violence

The involvement of security forces and lower-ranking members of the military in jihadist terrorism has also contributed to Pakistan's troubles with Islamist violence. The conflicting reports of Khaled Sheikh Mohammad's arrest certainly highlight the links that may have been established among al-Qaeda, radical Pakistani religious groups, and Pakistani security forces. According to some accounts, Mohammad was arrested along with an accomplice in the house of Ahmed Abdul Qudoos, the son of the leader of the Jamaat Islam (JI) women's league[62]—a key organization in the Muttahida Majlis-e-Amal (MMA) coalition of Islamist opposition groups,[63] and an important source of opposition to the Musharraf regime. Other accounts, meanwhile, suggest that he was arrested while a guest of a serving major in the Pakistan Army.[64] Several prominent Pakistani analysts believe that Mohammad was in fact being protected by the military officer but was planted in Qudoos's home both in an attempt to cover up the direct role of the officer and to create political problems for the JI. A September 2003 admission by the army itself added to this sense of confusion and suspicion about Mohammad's arrest. It affirmed that several midlevel officers, including a lieutenant colonel, had been arrested on charges of helping Mohammad and maintaining links to "Islamist extremist groups."[65] The military has since stated that al-Qaeda has never enjoyed support in its ranks beyond this tiny cell.[66]

However, over the last two years, there have been numerous published reports about the role of army and air force officers and enlisted personnel in the assassination attempts on Musharraf and the role of the police in the assassination attempt on Karachi Corps commander Hayat. The December 25, 2003, attack on Musharraf, for example, is widely thought to have involved lower-ranking members of the military and commandos drawn from the Special Services Group (SSG).[67] Military and civilian persons in the armed forces were reportedly recruited by Amjad Hussain Farooqui, a former member of JeM. Further, he is said to have provided training to the conspirators on December 14, less than two weeks before the failed attempt. Farooqui is known to have sheltered Mohammad, and after Mohammad's capture in March 2003, he began working with al-Libbi and Omar Saeed Shaikh.[68]

High-ranking officials in the Pakistan Army do not perceive these cases to be significant, arguing that many of those involved were either low-ranking officers (mostly captains), noncommissioned officers, or enlisted personnel.[69] However, the near success of these and other attempts to kill high-ranking leaders cooperating in the U.S.-led GWOT underscore that even relatively junior members of the military possess both the capability and skills to cause instability to the state. Reports of jihadist missionaries openly preaching within army facilities also raise questions about the general level of support enjoyed by al-Qaeda and other Islamist groups within the armed forces and the extent to which such support is tolerated within the wider institutional structure of the security forces.[70]

Impact on Pakistani Stability

Jihadist terrorism has had a decisive impact on Pakistan's internal stability. Most directly, it has emerged as a significant threat to Pakistan's leadership. As noted above, President Musharraf has already been the target of two concerted assassination attempts with the ostensible goal of provoking a national crisis that would topple the central government.[71] Potentially as serious are signs that groups operating in Kashmir, as well as the sectarian organization, Lashkar-e-Jhangvi (LeJ), have not only reoriented their focus but are also now acting in concert. The attack on French engineers in Karachi in 2002 exemplifies this union of effort, involving cadres from JeM and LeJ.[72] The future possibility of even closer and more tactically oriented links being forged among groups with different ideologies cannot be entirely dismissed.

Many Pakistani analysts believe that there has been an expansion of radical Islamist sentiment as a result of President Musharaff's efforts to bring about "enlightened moderation." These analysts argue that the country has become increasingly polarized and may soon loose any effective middle ground of compromise at least in part because the enlightened-moderation policy does not have much support beyond Pakistan's Islamabad-based elite.[73] In many ways this phenomenon is rooted in the machinations of Pakistan's domestic politics. The military has for decades used Islam in a highly utilitarian manner to legitimize its extraconstitutional role in government.[74] Similarly, the state's two historical mainstream parties, the Pakistan's People Party (PPP) and the Pakistan Muslim League (PML), have episodically struck Faustian bargains with Islamist organization to secure sufficient numbers in parliament to form a government.[75]

The 2002 elections, which brought the MMA to prominence, reflect some of these divisions within the Pakistani polity. This multiparty religious alliance politically dominates the NWFP and enjoys considerable support in Baluchistan. Further, the alliance, which is vigorously opposed to the GWOT and the modernist leanings of the federal government, has caused Islamabad a number of problems, not least by undermining the aforementioned efforts aimed at reforming and regulating *madaris* and wider attempts to rein in and curtail the activities of militant Islamists operating on the ground. More pointedly, the MMA, through its various activities, has helped spawn a radical environment that espouses policies fundamentally at odds with Musharaff's aim of progressively modernizing and moderating the country's domestic arena.

Jihadist extremism has also significantly complicated Islamabad's external relations, particularly with India. Delhi has repeatedly portrayed Pakistan as a bastion of Islamist extremism that poses a fundamental threat not only to the entire South Asian region but also—particularly in the wake of the 2005 London bombings—to the world. On a more direct level, the two states came close to an all-out war following the December 2001 assault on the Indian Parliament.[76] While Pakistan's official position is that Delhi "stage managed" the strike and the government steadfastly dismisses claims that Pakistan-backed Islamist militants were responsible for the assault, there are few commentators outside of Pakistan who accept this account. Indeed, certain analysts remain convinced that members of the ISI—perhaps of low to middle rank—not only knew about the operation but also may have provided some degree of logistical assistance for the attack.[77]

Regardless of the veracity of the various claims and counterclaims surrounding the attack, the 2001 assault clearly demonstrated that Pakistan's reliance upon proxy elements to prosecute its national-security strategy vis-à-vis India has had severe and negative consequences for the country's own national-security interests. That a situation of this sort should arise is especially unnerving given that both states possess nuclear weapons and that India has itself pursued an explicit limited-war doctrine since 1999 and a "cold-start" doctrine since 2002.[78]

Sectarian Violence

Scope, Dimensions and Causal Factors

Sectarian violence in Pakistan emanates from rival Sunni and Shi'a groups that have engaged in an increasingly bloody conflict since the mid-1980s.[79] The chief protagonists in this domestic interreligious rivalry include on the Sunni side the SSP and its terrorist offshoot the LeJ and on the Shi'a side the Tahrik-e-Jafaria (TJP) and its militant wing Sipah-e-Muhammad Pakistan (SMP).[80] The genesis of these groups can be traced back to two events in the late 1970s: (1) the program of Sunni Islamicization deliberately propagated by the regime of General Muhammad Zia ul-Haqq and (2) the 1979 Iranian Revolution.

Zia's Program of Islamicization

On assuming power in 1977, General Zia quickly moved to set in motion a broad-ranging Islamist agenda, which despite its claim to be reflective of universal Muslim values was, in fact, based on narrow Sunni interpretations of religious law.[81] Two elements were integral to this program—the establishment of a unified curriculum for Sunni and Shi'a students and the imposition of taxes on wealth (*zakat*) and agricultural produce (*usher*) that would be automatically collected from people's bank accounts.[82]

Pakistan's Shi'a community viewed these stipulations with fear and resentment and objected to them on two fronts. First, they believed that any joint educational curriculum would inevitably be slanted to promote the interests of the country's majority Sunni population.[83] And second, Shi'a interpretations of tax laws clearly specify that all levies should be voluntary, paid to representatives of the Shi'a imams (rather than the state), and calculated according to (Shi'a) *ja'fari fiqah* as opposed to (Sunni) *hanfi fiqah* jurisprudence—not least because the rate of tax for the former is lower than that of the latter.[84]

The Iranian Revolution, Domestic Policies, and the Rise of Sectarian
Militant Organizations

Zia's program of Islamicization coincided with the 1979 overthrow of the Shah of Iran by Ayatollah Khomeini. The ideological fervor behind this forced regime change, combined with the fact that the world's first Islamist revolution had not been carried out by Sunnis, had a direct impact on Pakistan's Shi'a community, politicizing their religious identity and emboldening the course of their sectarian mobilization vis-à-vis the country's Sunni majority.[85]

Throughout 1979–80, Shi'a groups organized major street protests against the government, culminating in an effective siege of Islamabad in July 1980 when more than 100,000 people blocked all traffic to the capital's ministries for three days. That same month, Mufti Ja'far Husayn formed the Tehrik-e-Nafaz Fiqh-e-Ja'fariyya (TNJF, literally the Movement for the Implementation of Ja'fari Fiqah—later renamed the TJF). The organization actively promoted and disseminated pro-Iranian literature throughout Pakistan that praised the virtues of Khomeini-like leaders in defending and promoting Shi'a interests. More importantly, the group was instrumental in forcing President Zia to recognize non-Sunni religious and communal rights—thus legitimizing sectarian posturing—and in extracting from him a pledge that the Shi'a would, henceforth, be exempted from all aspects of his Islamicization program that contravened *ja'fari fiqah*.[86]

The formation of the TNJF/TJF eventually led to the establishment of the SSP, a rival Sunni *tanzeem*, in 1984. The organization—which was founded by Maulana Haq Nawaz Jhangvi and led by Maulana Azam Tariq until his murder on October 6, 2003—was specifically created to battle the TJF at all levels and to marginalize its Shi'a base as being both non-Muslim and illegitimate. The SSP's goal is to establish a Pakistani state that is based on Sunni religious precepts and that both endorses and emulates the "rightly guided" caliphs of early Islam.[87]

While the TJF and SSP constitute the political framework for sectarian radicalism in Pakistan, the thrust of the ensuing violence has come from their respective militant wings: the SMP in the case of the former and the LeJ in the case of the latter.

SMP. Ghulum Raza Naqvi founded the SMP in the early 1990s (the exact date of the group's birth remains a matter of debate).[88] Born in the Khanewal district of the Punjab and a veteran of the anti-Soviet *mujahadeen* campaign in Afghanistan, Naqvi argued that the politically oriented nature of the TJF was preventing its younger cadres from physically countering and responding to Sunni attacks and harassment. Accordingly, while the group claims to promote broad Shi'a interests in the context of the right to religious freedom in Pakistan,[89] its main function has been to serve as a conduit for channeling and directing Shi'a extremism against the SSP and its various militant off-shoots.[90]

Indian sources estimate that the SMP is able to count on a base of roughly 30,000 followers, the vast majority of whom are from the Punjab, Karachi, and the NWFP. (This number could not be corroborated by non-Indian sources.) SMP members have typically studied at *madaris* across Pakistan—and not infrequently in Iran—and many are veterans of the anti-Soviet Afghan war. However, the group's training appears to be based solely in Pakistan[91] and there is no indication that SMP has sought to extend the range and scope of its active operations beyond Islamabad's territorial boundaries.[92]

LeJ. LeJ was founded in 1996 by a breakaway group of radical Sunni extremists—including Akram Lahori, Malik Ishaque, Riaz Basra, and Muhammad Ajmal—who reportedly believed that the SSP was deviating from the anti-Shi'a principles associated with Nawaz Jhangvi (from whom the organization derives its name) and that the only way to effectively promote Sunni interests in Pakistan was through violent means. LeJ has an estimated militant base of 300 members organized into semiautonomous cells of five to eight individuals. Most of its hardcore members are based in the Punjab.[93]

Both the SSP and LeJ maintain that they are in no way organizationally linked, though few analysts in India and Pakistan believe this to be the case. The two group's cadres come from the same Deobandi *madaris* and share the same sectarian belief system, worldview, and charter of demands. In addition, the SSP leadership has never overtly criticized the terrorist actions of LeJ. It is suspected that the latter merely serves as a cover through which the former can direct attacks against Shi'a and deny accountability.[94]

Impact on Pakistani Internal Stability

Sectarian violence has had a decisive impact on Pakistani stability. Between 2002 and 2004, 304 people were killed in Sunni-Shi'a clashes across the country (see table 1).[95] Assaults now routinely target hitherto sacrosanct religious sites, frequently involving suicide bombers who strike during heavily attended prayer sessions. Individuals have also been killed at home, in hospitals, and in funeral processions. While manifestations of mob violence have become less frequent in recent years (itself a sign of progress),[96] the attacks themselves have increased in scale.[97] This litany of violence has torn at communal relations in Pakistan, exacerbating an uncompromising retaliatory mindset that, as researchers Sundeep Waslekar, Leena Pillai, and Shabnam Siddiqui note, has radically weakened norms of even basic civility: "The increasing militarization and brutalization of the conflict has meant that there are virtually no sanctuaries left—neither at home, nor at the mosque, the hospital, or in jail. And being innocent is not the issue. Just 'being' is enough—being Shi'a or Sunni."[98]

The sectarian conflict has negatively interacted with other sources of insecurity in Pakistan, including, notably, organized crime and other forms of Islamist extremism. U.S. analysts believe that LeJ and SSP cadres pragmatically work with drug-trafficking syndicates, facilitating the movement of Afghan-sourced heroin across Pakistan's western borders and through its southern coast for both consumption within the country and dissemination to international markets.[99] Indian commentators and Pakistani journalists further contend that Sunni extremists have begun to take on more explicit antigovernment designs, which has manifested itself in high-level attacks on the country's leadership.[100]

Table 1. Deaths Resulting from Sunni-Shi'a Sectarian Violence, 2002–2004

Year	Violent Incidents	Deaths
2002	35	53
2003	13	80
2004	17	181

Source: Pakistan's Ministry of the Interior, January 2005.

The bloodshed and civil unrest that has been associated with the Sunni-Shi'a conflict has also fed into more generalized social instability by disrupting commercial trade, destroying infrastructure, and deterring overseas investment. In major hubs such as Karachi and smaller metropolitan centers in the Punjab, these effects have translated into chronic unemployment and poverty, triggering the growth of large, lawless slums and illegal squatter settlements that have themselves acted as major magnets for additional urban conflict.[101]

Drugs Trafficking

Scope, Dimensions, and Causal Factors

While Pakistan is officially part of the infamous South Asian Golden Crescent opium-producing arc,[102] it is really more of a major transit state for heroin (along with Iran and the Central Asian republics) than a source country in its own right.[103] The vast bulk of narcotics shipped through Pakistan is produced in Afghanistan, the world's principal supplier of opiates.[104] According to the U.S. Department of State, 2004 was a record year for Afghan poppy cultivation with roughly 206,700 hectares grown—more than treble the area devoted to the plant in 2003. Further, some 4,950 metric tons of opium gum was produced in Afghanistan in 2004, which represented a 35 percent increase over the previous high of 3,656 metric tons set in 1999 (see table 2) and exceeded the 292 metric tons produced by Burma, the second-largest producer, by a multiple of seventeen.[105] Several factors have accounted for the rapid increase in Afghan drug production, including:

❖ The overthrow of the Taliban regime in 2001 (Mullah Omar had placed a ban on poppy cultivation in 2000);[106]

❖ Alleged U.S. willingness to tolerate drug production during and immediately after OEF for wider geostrategic purposes;[107]

❖ The Afghan peasantry's overwhelming dependence on opium farming to access land, labor, and credit;[108]

❖ The inability of the Karzai transitional (and now elected) government to exercise concerted control over major crop growing regions in the country's Nangarhar, Helmand, Kandahar, and Oruzgan provinces.[109]

Western drug officials maintain that, on average, at least a quarter of the unrefined, refined, and morphine-based opiates produced in Afghanistan pass through Pakistan, which acts as a central conduit to both Turkey and Iran (the main hubs for the movement of narcotics to the European market). Overall volumes have steadily increased since 2001 in line with the expansion of the narcotics trade in Afghanistan, with a record 34 metric tons of heroin seized in Pakistan in 2003; this haul, which was the largest recorded by any country during that year, represented a 283 percent increase over 2002 figures and a massive 466 percent over 2001's total (see table 3).[110] This rise is due not only to increased trafficking but also to heightened border security in Iran and the provision of U.S. counter-narcotics assistance to Pakistani authorities.

The primary drug transit route in Pakistan runs through Baluchistan and the NWFP—where state penetration historically has not been strong[111]—and exits through ports on the largely unmonitored Makran coast,[112] international airports located in the country's major cities, or overland into Iran.[113] Available evidence suggests that illicit drugs are now being split into smaller, more numerous consignments that are easier to smuggle and less prone to single, large-scale seizures. Known as the "scatter-gun" approach, this method typically involves opiate packages of between 20 and 50 kilograms as opposed to the 1,000 kilogram shipments of several years ago.[114] Traffickers based in Quetta and Karachi organize most of these movements, coordinating their activities both with local sectarian groups—who use the profits to procure weapons—and subcontractors and brokers based in Turkey and Iran.[115]

Europe and, to a lesser extent, Russia constitute the main destination points for the bulk of the narcotics trafficked through Pakistan, and both are areas where the street value of heroin is high (particularly so in Europe).[116] In November 2004, the United Nations reported that European and Russian shipments had increased by 64 percent as compared to a year ago.[117] Remaining stocks of opiates in Pakistan are either couriered to secondary markets in India, Bangladesh, Sri Lanka, and eastern Africa—particularly Kenya, where Nigerian syndicates play a key role in arranging transshipments for consumption in South Africa—or remain in the country for indigenous consumption.[118]

Table 2. Afghan Opium Statistics, 1994–2004

	1994	1995	1996	1997	1998	1999	2000	2001	2002	2003	2004
Total Cultivation (in hectares)	29,180	38,740	37,950	39,150	41,720	51,500	64,510	1,685	30,750	61,000	206,700
Potential Yield (in metric tons)	950	1,250	2,099	2,184	2,340	2,861	3,656	74	1,278	2,865	4,950

Source: Office of International Narcotics and Law Enforcement Affairs, "Afghanistan," in International Narcotics Control Strategy Report, 2005 (Washington, D.C.: U.S. Department of State, March 2005).

Note: Potential yield estimates for 1996–1999 have been revised upward from previous International Narcotics Control Strategy Reports, reflecting improved methodologies for estimating opium yields.

Table 3. Opiate Seizures and Drug Arrests in Pakistan, 1996–2004

	1996	1997	1998	1999	2000	2001	2002	2003	2004
Opium (in metric tons)	8.08	8.54	5.02	16.32	7.84	5.2	2.4	5.4	2.5
Heroin (in metric tons)	4.05	5.07	3.33	4.98	7.41	6.0	8.9	34.0	24.7
Arrests	51,119	50,565	37,745	45,175	35,969	—	—	46,346	49,186

Source: Adapted from Office of Narcotics and International Law Enforcement Affairs, "Pakistan," in International Narcotics Control Strategy Report, 2003 and 2005.

* In metric tons

Pakistan's emergence as an important transit point for heroin reflects both the country's geostrategic location and the extremely porous and unregulated nature of its land and sea borders.[119] In addition, weak legal and regulatory financial systems in Pakistan engender an environment highly conducive to organized illicit activities in at least three ways: (1) it allows crime syndicates to bypass official arrest and prosecution procedures and to corrupt the very highest levels of political and judicial power; (2) it permits the laundering of heroin profits transmitted via the official banking system;[120] and (3) it enables the rapid and covert movement of funds through informal channels, particularly the *hawala* network (explained in greater detail below).

Impact on Pakistani Security

The opium trade has had a marked effect on Pakistani security and stability in a number of ways. First, it has contributed to a growing public health and addiction problem. According to one domestic survey undertaken in 2004, there are between 3.5 and 5 million habitual—as opposed to recreational—drug users in the country, at least 500,000 of whom are chronic heroin abusers. The overall prevalence of chronic users, expressed in terms of the whole population, is roughly a third of one percent—a ratio that is among the highest in the world. Habitual users, meanwhile, comprise about 3 percent of the population.[121] The drug problem is particularly acute in the Punjab, which accounts for some 45 percent of this total. However, an estimated 60 percent of Pakistanis have been affected in one way or another by the drug trade, either directly or as a result of the wider debilitating social effects it has on extended family relationships.

Opiate abuse accounts for a growing proportion of the country's total drug use—currently as much as 7 percent—as more and more people switch to it from hashish, charas, and other narcotic substances.[122] These figures give particular cause for alarm when one considers that Pakistan has a maximum capacity to treat only around 7,600 drug users per year—a fraction of the country's present addict population. On the basis of current trends, this mismatch between drug abuse and rehabilitation resources will only increase, leaving Islamabad exposed to a disquieting pull-push dynamic that, through the laws of supply and demand, will result in growing volumes of opiates ending up on the country's streets.[123]

Apart from addiction, intravenous (IV) heroin use has fostered the spread of the Human Deficiency Virus (HIV), the causative agent for Acquired Immunodeficiency Syndrome (AIDS). Officials with Pakistan's National AIDS Control Program (NACP) reported in 2004 that the prevalence rate of HIV/AIDS among drug addicts had increased to 7.6 percent from 0.4 percent the previous year and that it was expected to rise significantly over the next several years in line with increased Afghan opiate production. The NACP revealed that, currently, 12 percent of the country's addicts inject heroin—or other poly-drug "cocktails"—and that the sharing of needles in so-called "shooting galleries" is both common and increasing, especially in Lahore and Karachi.[124] These latter findings endorsed the results of two earlier baseline studies undertaken by the United Nations, which showed a rapidly rising trend of multiple IV drug abuse during the 1990s.[125] International health experts have begun to pay greater attention to the worsening drug-disease nexus in Pakistan, warning that a runaway immunodeficiency problem may be looming on the horizon.[126] Delegates at an AIDS awareness conference held in Islamabad during January 2005 universally agreed that Pakistan now constituted "a high (as opposed to a potentially high) HIV epidemic country."[127]

Second, the opium trade has contributed to growing social instability by fueling high rates of drug-related crime among both users struggling to finance their habit and traffickers and distributors striving to gain control of a greater share of the narcotics market. As highlighted in table 3, law enforcement officials arrested 46,346 individuals on drug-related charges in 2003—a 77 percent increase from the 2000 total (figures for 2001 and 2002 are not available).[128] Arguably more problematic, however, has been the emergence of extremely powerful drug syndicates within Pakistan. The country's most influential entity in this regard is the Karachi mafia, which controls most of the international conduits used to transport not only South Asian opiates but also weapons and explosives. Dawood Ibrahim, an Indian-born smuggler of gold and other high-value assets, is believed to act as the main link in the syndicate's operations in Bombay, Karachi, and Dubai.[129] Indian intelligence and law enforcement sources maintain that Ibrahim's trafficking channels were employed by terrorists to bring in the arms and explosives (RDX) that were used in the series of coordinated blasts in Bombay in 1993. While Tiger Memon, an associate of Ibrahim, is believed to have been the chief logistical operator of the attacks, Indian officials believe that Ibrahim was the "mastermind" without whose help the operation could not have proceeded.[130]

Third, the opium trade has contributed to growing economic instability due to the costs associated with trying to control opium imports. That is, the diversion of scarce resources to counternarcotics efforts has weakened an already fragile economy. Internal drug prevention and reduction initiatives planned for Pakistan over the next three years are expected to exceed half a billion dollars.[131] This represents a considerable burden for a country whose gross domestic product (GDP) in 2003 amounted to only $295.3 billion and whose unemployment rates run to around 8 percent, which is on top of substantial—but not well quantified—underemployment rates.[132]

Finally, money from illicit heroin sales has contributed to instability by encouraging corruption in the official government sector. According to a 2004 report by Transparency International (TI), law enforcement personnel and members of the judiciary are among the most corrupt elements of the Pakistani establishment. Police officers and judges have been repeatedly singled out for their willingness to establish mutually beneficial working partnerships with drug dealers—as well as other criminal syndicates—to offset inadequate pay, insufficient pension and public service provision, and the growing demands of increasingly large families.[133]

These effects of the opium trade have collectively had an adverse impact on Pakistan's overall domestic viability, undermining both institutional state development and legitimate economic enterprise. Further, corruption, crime, and economic stagnation in Pakistan deprive Washington of a strong ally that could help stem drug flows from Afghanistan, offset the burden of U.S. counternarcotics efforts in South Asia, and mitigate the perception that the regional drug war is being pursued purely for unilateral U.S. interests.

Goods Smuggling and Human Trafficking

Scope, Dimensions, and Causal Factors

Illicit smuggling is pervasive in Pakistan; everything from tea, clothes, chinaware, and electronics to car parts, oil, and petroleum products are sold in black-market bazaars (or *baras*, as they are known in Pakistan) located along the country's porous border with Afghanistan.[134] Most of these goods originate from manufacturers located in Central Asia, the Middle East, and the Persian Gulf (particularly Iran) and are brought into the country through the exploitation of arrangements instituted under the Afghan Transit Trade Agreement (ATTA).[135] The World Bank estimates the value of this "stealth" economy at more than $30 billion, roughly a tenth of the country's official GDP, one of the highest ratios in the world.[136]

The *hawala*—a network of finance brokers and lenders who transmit funds to and from Pakistan without physically moving money across borders or creating a paper trail—was formerly at the heart of much of this underground trade. In 2002, the U.S.-based Citigroup noted that *hawala* flows into Pakistan were so robust that the national economy was becoming dependent on the inputs provided by this parallel macro-fiscal universe, while Pakistani Central Bank officials believed that six men based in Karachi and Dubai—all members of the Memon ethnic group—sat at the apex of this informal remittance system, acting as a de facto "mafia" whose mutually supportive contacts stretched from Peshawar to New York.[137] However, in 2002, Pakistan undertook massive efforts to channel these *hawala* funds through official financial institutions. As a consequence, Pakistan's exchequer has benefited tremendously from the rerouting of these resources; the record-breaking cash remittance figures for fiscal year 2002–03 demonstrated the impact of the global *hawala* crackdown and Pakistan's own efforts.[138]

The country has also emerged as a major source, destination, and transshipment point for human trafficking, particularly for women and girls sold into prostitution and bonded labor, for children sent to the Middle East to become camel jockeys, and for adolescent boys forcibly recruited from local *madaris* to fight in Afghanistan. The true extent of this human trade is unknown, although the FIA claims to receive, on average, five reports a day of attempts to illegally move people through the country.[139]

Washington currently includes Pakistan on its human trafficking Tier 2 Watch List, meaning that the country does not fully meet the minimum requirements of the U.S. Trafficking Victims Act[140] and that it has provided no evidence over the previous year that it has increased efforts to comply with this act.[141] Should this situation continue, Islamabad risks possible targeted sanctions and international opprobrium by being assigned

Tier 3 status—the lowest designation accorded by the U.S. Department of State's Office to Monitor and Combat Trafficking in Persons.[142]

Several factors account for this profusion of smuggling and trafficking activity inside Pakistan, including:

❖ Long—and in some cases porous—land borders with Afghanistan, India, Iran, and China

❖ Ineffective and insufficient coastal surveillance, particularly around the Port of Karachi, which remains one of the main trade outlets connecting South Asia with the Middle East and Africa (This concern will be extended to include the port at Gwadar on the Baluch coast as it comes online over the next few years.)[143]

❖ Restrictions or prohibitions of certain goods entering the country

❖ High import duties

❖ Corrupt customs and immigration inspectors, who are often complicit in smuggling rackets (This is something that has been especially problematic at checkpoints along the Grand Truck [GT] Road between Islamabad and Rawalpindi and Peshawar.)

❖ A geographic and strategic location that straddles routes to and from West, East, and Central Asia

❖ A large immigrant population of 7 million (according to FIA figures) that comes from fifteen South and Central Asian countries

❖ An entrenched cash culture[144] predicated on tax avoidance[145]

Impact on Internal Pakistani Stability

The implications of this illicit trade in humans and goods are complex and multifaceted. First, and most directly, commodity smuggling robs the country of billions of dollars a year. According to the World Bank, petroleum product smuggling alone costs Pakistan some Rs 5–6 billion per year in forfeited taxes and duty.[146] Further, the annual underground trade in car and truck tires during the 1990s was conservatively thought to be in the range of Rs 2.1 billion, while annual losses from smuggled cigarettes currently amount to roughly Rs 75 million.[147]

Second, and directly related to the above, illicit commodity exchanges have severely strained the viability of local businesses and industries to the extent that many cannot compete with their underground counterparts. A case in point is the national tea industry, which over the last two to three years has been progressively sidelined by the underground sector. In 2003, an estimated 40,000 megatons of tea was smuggled into Pakistan out of a total of 130,000 megatons imported into the country. These unregulated imports have not only undercut the fabric of legitimate tea growers and producers but also generated pressure to slash protective custom tariffs from 25 percent to just 10 percent in an effort to offset the relative price attractiveness of illegal sales.[148]

Third, consumer smuggling has exacerbated the politically corrosive effects of the drugs trade by engendering and entrenching bureaucratic corruption. It is now standard practice for owners and drivers of buses traveling along the GT Road—most of which are loaded with an assortment of undeclared goods—to offer bribes to customs, excise, and police officials manning checkpoints en route to Islamabad, while brokers on the Karachi Stock Exchange regularly cooperate with government departments and intelligence agencies in laundering money generated from the country's black economy.[149] The pervasiveness of corruption has had a negative impact on Pakistan's nascent democratic experiment, not least by fostering a general disregard for law and order among broad sections of the civilian population. Indeed, many Pakistanis regard the criminal justice system as oppressive and believe it serves solely the interests of those who abuse it for their own selfish designs.[150]

Finally, profits from the human trade have fuelled an already booming underground economy, provided capital for other associated illicit activities, such as documentation forgery, and galvanized the growth of human-trafficking rings, many of which have moved to establish links with other transnational criminals, such as arms dealers, drug syndicates, and jihadist groups. Due to a lack of resources, a failure to adequately distinguish between trafficked and smuggled persons, and ordinance laws that effectively equate rape with consensual sex,[151] Pakistan's victim-assistance efforts are minimal at best, meaning that even if a trafficked individual does return home eventually, he or she is likely to turn to crime for self-sustenance and survival. Just as significant, the abduction of children and adolescents has undermined the basic right of all persons to be free from sexual abuse and exploitation. It has also interrupted the passage of knowledge and cultural values from generation to generation, significantly weakening the communal and family relationships that lie at the root of any functioning civil society.[152]

While not directly impacting on U.S. security interests, the smuggling of goods and the trafficking of humans—as with the drug trade—erodes the cornerstones of economic, social, and political stability in Pakistan. This not only limits Pakistan's ability to be a full partner in Washington's regional security-building activities, but it also fosters a dysfunctional internal environment that—as Afghanistan, Central Asia, and parts of Africa bear witness—can be easily exploited by regional extremists for logistical and funding purposes.

Corruption

Scope, Dimensions, and Causal Factors

Corruption has emerged as a notable feature of Pakistan's internal landscape.[153] However, the problem extends well beyond contingencies associated with the drugs trade and illicit smuggling, filtering out to most aspects of national life. Over the last ten years, the country has consistently been ranked in the upper 10 percent of TI's Corruption Perception Index (CPI),[154] with scores ranging between 2.1 to 2.7 (out of a possible maximum "clean" of 10).[155] TI's surveys of academics, businesspeople, risk analysts, and ordinary citizens reveal a startling picture, highlighting a state in which many of the most important arms of government are perceived to be rife with graft and institutionalized dishonesty.

TI's 2003 report on Pakistan details the results of its countrywide survey in which respondents were asked their perceptions of relative corruption levels in seven major areas government. Specifically, 3,000 respondents were asked to identify which arm of government was, in their view, the most corrupt. The largest number of respondents (27.7 percent) identified the police as being most corrupt, followed by the power sector (15.3 percent), and tax department (12.7 percent). NGOs, post offices, and banks were least likely to be identified as the "most corrupt" arm of government (see table 4). Tellingly, the survey also revealed that the services recognized as being "most utilized" by the population were those offered by the police (32 percent), the power sector (17 percent), and the taxation department (13 percent).[156]

Table 4. Most Corrupt Sectors in Pakistan according to Public Opinion

Sector	Percentage*
Police	27.68
Power	15.26
Taxation	12.69
Judiciary	9.54
Customs	8.56
Health	5.41
Land	5.18
Education	3.38
Telephone	2.24
Railway	1.24
NGOs	0.39
Post Office	0.31
Bank	0.19
Others**	7.93
Total	100.00

Source: Transparency International Country Study Report–Pakistan 2003, 27–28.

* Percentages are based on a survey sample of 3,000; each individual surveyed was asked to identify the sector that was "most corrupt."

** Others included the passport office, identification card issuance centers, the Attorney Generals Department, and political parties.

This study further found that bribes are routinely paid for any number of things, such as for being relieved of a traffic fine, ensuring connectivity to an electricity supply, having a case heard by a sympathetic judge, securing access to medical care, settling land disputes, and altering exam results.[157]

Determining the extent of monies paid to corrupt officials is difficult to ascertain, largely because in most cases those involved are reluctant to disclose the true amount of the payoff. However, conservative estimates put total annual consumer "expenditure" on bribes at between $2 and $4 billion, with the biggest payouts accruing to the Judiciary and the Land,

Education, and Tax Departments (see table 5). One retired chief justice of Pakistan's Supreme Court went so far as to state that Pakistan's principal problem is corruption, maintaining that Pakistan's "economy has gone down because of deep rooted corruption in society . . . from bureaucrats and others." "Eliminating corruption is crucial," he added. "Any change to be brought about in the country . . . must address corruption and accountability."[158] Alarmingly, most citizens appear to accept corruption as an unavoidable fact of life, resigning themselves to a system that is viewed as largely unfixable. Indeed, the majority of Pakistanis do not have any sense of entitlement to accountability and justice from their public institutions.[159]

The roots and causes of corruption in Pakistan reflect a variety of inter-related historical, cultural, economic, and institutional factors. Part of the problem stems from the entrenched feudalism that transcends the national society; blood ties and clan and tribal loyalties trump respect for the state and its legal institutions. More specifically, feudal family structures and related political alliances have prevented the development of what might

Table 5. Average Bribe per Sector

Sector	Number Of Respondents Who Reported Paying A Bribe	Total Amount Of Bribes (In Rs)	Average Bribe (In Rs)
Police	614	1,430,975	2,231
Power	296	321,765	1,087
Tax	256	987,695	3,858
Health	227	176,476	777
Education	132	635,023	4,811
Land Administration	151	907,921	6,013
Judiciary	108	1,044,368	9,670
Total	1,784	5,504,223	

Source: Adapted from Transparency International Country Study Report–Pakistan 2003, 28.

Notes: The second column indicates how many of the 1,784 survey respondents paid bribes in each sector in the previous year. The third column indicates the total amount of bribes paid by the respondents in each sector in the previous year. The fourth column provides the average bribe paid in each sector. With 1,784 people paying a total of Rs 5.5 million in bribes, each respondent paid on average Rs 3,085 in bribes over the course of the year.

otherwise have been a fairly progressive ruling urban elite. Instead, these structures and alliances are reflected in the failure of successive governments to carry out meaningful land reform and in the power that has been concentrated in the hands of an increasingly wealthy industrialist clique.[160]

A highly politicized bureaucracy that promotes on the basis of patronage rather than merit is exacerbating the situation. Further, the authority and power vested in civil servants propagates a perception that administrative posts "entitle" incumbents to perks and privileges. Low rates of pay relative to the private sector, nepotism, the will of individuals to pay "speed" money to expedite the filing of paperwork, and a general lack of individual accountability fuel this sense of entitlement, resulting in a system that in the words of one 1999 pilot study "thrives on the social utility of greed."[161] Little has changed since 1999, largely because the closed and insulated nature of the bureaucracy has stymied even limited efforts aimed at reform.[162]

Problems are equally serious, if not more so, in the judiciary. According to a recent ICG report, the executive exercises blatant control over the courts through a "system of judicial appointments, promotions and removals to ensure its allies fill key posts." For instance, following the October 1999 coup that brought Musharraf to power, judges who opposed the military's unconstitutional assumption of the presidency were systematically purged from the judiciary.[163] New judges must also be wary because the executive can remove them after one or two years by declining to "confirm" their appointments. This has effectively resulted in a court system staffed with political appointees who will toe the government's line and tolerate military rule.[164] Moreover, the executive ensures the loyalty of favored sitting judges through various indirect "reward" channels, such as granting the right to rent-free residences, positively altering other benefits and emoluments, guaranteeing secure postretirement income, and providing access to sought-after federal government positions beyond mandated retirement ages.[165] Corruption within the Subordinate Judiciary is even more blatant and revolves largely around direct litigant bribery of district and session judges who currently suffer from abysmally low salaries.[166] Indeed, it is allegedly not uncommon for clients to ask whether a judge can be bought off before ascertaining exactly where their case stands on its merits.[167]

Pervasive government involvement in commercial activity has also undoubtedly served to entrench and perpetuate corrupt practices. Although the economy is now more open than in the past, it continues to be highly regulated with many public corporations wielding monopolistic power in the absence of proper oversight, making them largely immune to private-sector competition and efficiencies. As TI explains, this intrusive regime of business control has both created and expanded incentives and opportunities for corruption. While macro-level regulations, such as quotas, subsidies, and price ceilings, do not lead to direct physical intrusion by the government, they do induce corruption among senior-level business managers.[168]

A final causal factor in the country's culture of corruption revolves around the extremely prominent role that the armed forces play in the running of the state. The military, which has remained at the apex of the state's power structure since independence—either in the form of direct rule (for nearly thirty years in total) or through influence over the presiding civilian administration[169]—has gone to decisive lengths to protect its preeminent and privileged political status, often at the expense of institutions designed to ensure accountable, clean, and democratic government. In 2003, for instance, Javed Hashimi, a prominent opposition figure who leads the Alliance for the Restoration of Democracy (ARD) and who has been one of the most vocal and consistent critics of the army's 1999 seizure of political power, was arrested on what have been widely denigrated as trumped-up charges of treason.[170] Even more indicative of the military's power and influence has been the judiciary, which has consistently ruled in favor of Islamabad in contravention of the intent of the law and, frequently, its own rulings. Indeed, in 2002, the Supreme Court Bar Association (SCBA) issued an unprecedented communiqué asserting that "attempting to argue a case before the present judiciary was a futile exercise because it had ceased to be politically independent and was now in a position of full subservience to the country's army rulers."[171]

The military has had an equally negative impact on the workings of the National Accountability Bureau (NAB), which operates under the National Accountability Ordinance of 1999 and was created to spearhead the government's anticorruption drive.[172] All three of the bureau's chairmen since its inception have been serving army generals[173] who have systematically exploited their broad-ranging powers[174] to target and discredit politicians out of favor with the regime in Islamabad. In addition, the military has vigorously ensured that serving army officers are isolated from wider NAB scrutiny and that judges are completely excluded from it. Reflecting this fact, as of August 2004, only twelve of the 695 cases filed by the bureau were brought against armed forces personnel and none were brought against the judiciary.[175] This pro-establishment bias has led many to view the NAB as an extension of the military and an agency that essentially gauges the salience of corruption investigations on the basis of vested self-interest and political calculations.[176]

Impact on Internal Pakistani Stability

The most visible effects of corruption on Pakistani internal stability have been economic in nature. For example, corruption has caused the public exchequer to lose out on approximately 64 percent, 48 percent, and 45 percent of possible revenue from income tax, customs, and sales tax, respectively. If accurate, this would represent an overall revenue shortfall of around Rs 200 billion ($3.3 billion) per annum—a loss the country can ill afford.[177]

Development projects have been particularly hard-hit, with key social investment choices and decisions on geographic location frequently influenced by private benefit considerations rather than empirically validated and community-based needs assessments. The inevitable result has been that human capital indicators—particularly literacy rates and educational levels[178]—have remained largely stagnant over the last decade and are currently among the worst in South Asia. Moreover, overseas aid that has not been put to productive use has saddled the country with a large external debt—the servicing of which currently runs at approximately 40 percent of overall budgetary expenditure. This has squeezed out, among other things, adequate remuneration for the public sector.[179]

The intrusive and unaccountable nature of "political business" has also stifled the emergence of efficient and vibrant commercial enterprise not only by eliminating competition but also by creating market uncertainty and engendering a general climate in which the inviolability of contracts cannot be guaranteed—significantly heightening problems associated with risk management and forecasting. Corruption within the legal system—

particularly in the subordinate courts—has compounded the situation, offering small- and medium-sized companies little, if any, standardized protection. Combined, these effects have crippled private-sector development, inhibited commercial transactions by heightening business uncertainty, encouraged massive waste, and increased costs to consumers.[180]

Further, as noted above, corruption has directly contributed to the growth of organized crime in Pakistan, "positively" impacting on the drugs trade, commodity smuggling, and human trafficking. This has engendered a civilian mindset that views and accepts illegality as the fast track to success (gangsters in cities such as Karachi are often accorded respect on account of the wealth they wield). Corruption has also contributed to the general degradation of the criminal justice system—key elements of which are often complicit in illegal enterprises. This has, in turn, reduced popular confidence in the legitimacy and enforcement capacity of the state and encouraged individuals to seek justice through extrajudicial measures.

Conclusion

As this chapter has described, Pakistan is currently plagued by a plethora of internal security and governance challenges. The effect of this destabilizing mosaic has been decisive, negatively affecting the formal leadership pillars of the central government, the political and economic foundations that are so integral to any functioning modern state, and the social fabric of the country. While many of these threats do not directly impact on U.S. security interests, they do represent a subset of the types of problems that the Bush administration has emphasized as being directly relevant to wider considerations of national and international security. Because Islamabad lacks a robust domestic law enforcement structure and civic administration to ameliorate these adverse conditions, they continue to thrive and expand in the country's permissive environment. More disturbing is evidence that elements of the state itself contribute to and foster conditions of corruption and criminality. As a result of this situation and the critical role the country currently plays in U.S. foreign and security policy, Pakistan has been the focus of concerted and growing U.S. aid programs designed to augment and fortify its internal resilience. The scope and parameters of these efforts are detailed in chapter 2.

2

U.S. Assistance Programs
to Pakistan

Introduction

The United States has devoted substantial resources to Pakistan as part of the GWOT. The centerpiece of this support—deemed critical to ensuring that Islamabad is able to play a meaningful role in combating al-Qaeda and associated jihadist threats—is a five-year, $3 billion assistance package. This funding, which requires congressional approval in each of the five years, amounts to $600 million annually, a sum that is evenly split between foreign military financing (FMF)[1] and economic support funds (ESF). The main purpose of this backing is to lay the groundwork for a long-term, mutually beneficial relationship that fosters and consolidates an internal environment in Pakistan hostile to Islamist extremism—one of the key recommendations of *The 9/11 Commission Report*.[2]

In addition to the FMF and EMS package, the United States has devoted funds to help fortify Pakistan's internal security apparatus, targeting specific counterterrorism, law enforcement, and governance initiatives.[3] Channeled primarily through the U.S. Department of State and the Department of Justice, these funds approximated $100 million in FY05—bringing total U.S. assistance for the year to $700 million.[4]

Pakistan has complemented U.S. assistance with its own efforts to upgrade law enforcement and internal security, passing, for example, Police Ordinance 2002, which repealed the former, anachronistic colonial Police Act of 1861.[5] Perhaps of greater import, high-level officials within Pakistan's MoI have argued forcefully for the need to reform and revamp the overall police and judicial infrastructure.[6] A principal component of these advocacy efforts involved soliciting U.S. assistance to help strengthen the state's law enforcement capacity. To this end, former interior minister Moinuddin Haider played a key role in helping to convene a Joint Working Group on Counter Terrorism and Law Enforcement (JWG-CTLE).

The group's inaugural meeting was held in Washington, D.C., in May 2002 and covered a range of issues, including counternarcotics, counterterrorism, money laundering, human trafficking, demand reduction for illegal substances, alternative development proposals, poppy eradication, police and legal system reform, the repatriation of Pakistani nationals held on visa violations, and the rendering of suspected terrorists.[7] Since then, the JWG-CTLE has met two times—once in Washington, D.C., in April 2003 and once in Islamabad seventeen months later—emerging as a key conduit for U.S.-Pakistani internal security collaboration.[8]

While all U.S. agencies working in Pakistan are guided by the strategic principles identified in *The 9/11 Commission Report,*[9] the provision of civilian security assistance to Pakistan is directed toward achieving four interrelated objectives:

1. Bolstering Pakistan's counterterrorism capabilities

2. Fortifying policy instruments that can be brought to bear against those criminal and other enterprises that support militant radicalism

3. Addressing the underlying dearth of security and governance that creates a permissive environment for extremism

4. Enabling the national government to effectively project authority and the rule of law throughout its national territory[10]

This chapter will outline those U.S. programs that are directly designed to assist Pakistan in dealing with the multifarious internal security threats detailed in chapter 1. It will identify the primary agencies involved in the programs and lay out the programs' principal objectives and assessments.

U.S. Agencies' Strategies and Challenges

The bulk of U.S. internal security assistance programs to Pakistan are run through the Department of State or the Department of Justice.

U.S. Department of State

There are several entities within the U.S. Department of State that are involved in providing internal security assistance (or "civilian security assistance" in the parlance of the State Department) to Pakistan. The bulk of these entities fall under the auspices of the Bureau of International Narcotics and Law Enforcement (INL), although several other State Department agencies also provide varying levels of assistance to them. Each agency has its own set of objectives and challenges with regard to Pakistan.

The INL

From the perspective of the INL, Pakistan represents a challenging tasking theater. Much of the terrain in which the INL currently operates is rugged, remote, and characterized by porous borders with many largely inaccessible frontier tribal belts. The INL regards areas such as Baluchistan and FATA as being largely bereft of central government authority and as providing viable havens and sanctuaries for terrorists, militants, and traffickers alike. In addition, the INL views the country's law enforcement and criminal justice system as weak, characterizing it as being "hollow . . . with limited resources and poor training . . . [and adversely affected by] interagency competition."[11] The INL states that these structural issues are further complicated by seemingly opaque domestic political divisions and opposition within Pakistan's government. Further, severe limitations upon U.S. mission staffing due to the prevailing Pakistani security environment make the provision of assistance difficult.[12]

Despite these conditions, the INL hopes to do the following in Pakistan:

1. Strengthen Islamabad's control of the Pakistan-Afghanistan border and expand central government access to the border areas to deny sanctuary to militant elements

2. Improve Pakistani law enforcement capacity and interagency cooperation

3. Enhance the country's counternarcotics capabilities[13]

After the 9/11 attacks and the subsequent launch of OEF, the INL received $73 million in supplemental funding to help fortify Pakistan's border areas. By way of comparison, prior to FY01, allocations to the INL for Pakistan totaled less than $2 million per year. While funding for this purpose has fallen off somewhat since 2001, it remains substantial, with $30.5 million apportioned in FY04 and $40 million requested in FY05.[14]

The S/CT and the DS/ATA

The U.S. Department of State Counterterrorism Office (S/CT) and the Bureau of Diplomatic Security, Office of Antiterrorism Assistance (DS/ATA) are also involved in efforts to enhance Pakistan's internal security. Programs instituted through these two agencies are inherently linked: the S/CT provides policy guidance and funding to the DS/ATA, which in turn implements the respective initiatives on the ground. The S/CT determines the relative priority of select countries for receiving specific kinds of training.[15]

S/CT officials have identified two main goals for its programs in Pakistan: (1) to foster Islamabad's *will* to meaningfully engage in the GWOT and (2) to provide Pakistan with the *tools* to decisively confront militant extremist threats emanating from within its borders. Compared to those of other agencies, the S/CT's budget for Pakistan is somewhat small, amounting to only $10 million in FY05. Most of these monies are directed toward enhancing Pakistan's basic investigative capabilities. In the view of S/CT officials, the only Pakistani agency that has an expertise in basic investigative techniques is the ISI, which is primarily an army-directed agency. It is the objective of the S/CT, therefore, to develop investigative skills within the *civilian* sector.

Most S/CT officials readily agree that Pakistan is prepared to actively engage *foreign* militants in the country, acknowledging that some of Islamabad's most tenacious counterterrorism efforts have been directed against Arabs, Uzbeks, and Chechens. In this regard, their general assessment is that Pakistan has done "amazing things" for the United States in the GWOT, especially when considering the lack of significant action by Pakistan against al-Qaeda and the Taliban prior to 9/11.[16] That said, certain S/CT officials question the full sincerity of Islamabad's stance on Islamist extremism, arguing that the central government continues to exhibit reticence when it comes to targeting its own nationals, particularly Pakhtuns in the FATA and NWFP and Islamist militants fighting in J&K.[17]

It is the view of the authors, however, that Pakistan has been more forthright in its stance on terrorism than these officials believe. Islamabad certainly appears to have become more attuned to the potential challenge "from within," particularly since Pakistanis were directly implicated in the various assassination attempts on Musharraf, Aziz, and Hayat. Indeed, since 2003, the central government has actively moved to arrest citizens believed to be linked to al-Qaeda or involved in plots against high-level leadership.[18]

While the DS/ATA takes its policy guidance from the S/CT, a country can participate in DS/ATA assistance programs only if it meets the following criteria:

❖ The state is categorized as existing in a condition of critical or high-level threat, is deemed to be incapable of meeting terrorist contingencies with its own resources, and hosts a substantial U.S. presence.

❖ The country is the last point of departure for airline flights to the United States.

❖ There are important bilateral policy interests at stake.[19]

Once these criteria have been met, a DS/ATA assessment team will work in conjunction with the DS/ATA's training board to develop a comprehensive country plan that covers training needs, courses, and equipment for the state in question. In developing the plan, the DS/ATA focuses on five key areas that it sees as fundamental to any nation's defense against terrorism. Specifically, these are aimed at ensuring the country has the ability (1) to enforce the law, preserve the peace, and safeguard life and property; (2) to protect the national leadership, seat and function of government, and the resident diplomatic corps in the country; (3) to control national borders; (4) to defend critical infrastructure; and (5) to manage crises that have national import.[20]

Once approved, the country plan goes to the program management branch for implementation. Programs are designed to provide the critical skills that are identified as lacking in the police and internal security forces and are aimed at improving functional performance, mid-level supervision, senior-level management, and leadership. The DS/ATA does not provide basic police training—the provision of which remains under the notional purview of the Islamabad government.[21]

In Pakistan, the main thrust of S/CT and DS/ATA training and development has centered on the following:

❖ The establishment of a dedicated Counterterrorism Special Investigation Group (SIG) at the national police academy in Rawalpindi (which accounted for the bulk of the $10 million allocated in FY05)

❖ The provision of dedicated courses in special weapons and tactics (SWAT), VIP/diplomatic protection, and weapons of mass destruction (WMD) response

❖ The institution of a comprehensive framework for border security, surveillance command, and control in the NWFP[22]

USAID

After a seven-year hiatus precipitated by Pakistan's nuclear tests in 1998, the United States Agency for International Development (USAID) returned to Pakistan in June 2002 to "tangibly improve the lives of the poor in [the country] and to build support for [Islamabad's] decision to join the international war on terrorism and thwart further terrorist recruiting."[23] Overall, USAID provided some $147.6 million (in FY05) to Pakistan, which was used to improve the country's education and health sectors; create employment and economic opportunities; and strengthen governance. While the largest commitment was in the education sector ($67 million in FY05), USAID also planned to spend at least $13 million to help bolster the transparency of the nation's electoral and legislative processes.[24]

In addition, USAID is actively contributing to the INL's efforts in FATA by constructing schools there. This work is being coordinated with Pakistan in an effort both to win the "hearts and minds" of the local residents and to open up the tribal areas so that they can be integrated into the mainstream of the Pakistani state.[25]

U.S. Department of Justice

Department of Justice security assistance to Pakistan takes place through the International Criminal Investigative Training Assistance Program (ICITAP) and the Drug Enforcement Agency (DEA).

ICITAP

ICITAP, which coordinates its work with the INL,[26] has identified several problems specific to its core mission in Pakistan. First, several of the law enforcement agencies that operate on the country's borders and adjacent areas[27] lack training and equipment and have inadequate communication capabilities. Second, many of these agencies are overworked and insufficiently coordinated, which negatively affects their overall effectiveness as professional law enforcement institutions. Third, the topography of Pakistan's western borders, the dearth of roads and other infrastructure in the tribal areas, and the region's tenacious support for al-Qaeda and Taliban elements have dramatically complicated the ability of extant law enforcement agencies to fulfill effectively their statutory mandates.[28]

ICITAP has also highlighted other impediments to the effective delivery and long-term viability of its programs. Specifically, these pertain to "the absorptive capacity of the organizations receiving the training, loss of tacit knowledge and sustainability resulting from [staff] rotations, commitment of personnel, [and] operational integration and mission . . . caps."[29] Moreover, ICITAP has noted that because Pakistan's law enforcement officers are severely underpaid (with the arguable exception of the motorway police), they remain "susceptible to outside influences and corruption, and are not respected by the public."[30] Additionally, Justice Department officials deride the country's law enforcement agencies' critically low organizational investigative ratio, which currently stands at just 12 percent—that is, 12 percent of officers are capable of undertaking substantive investigative activities[31]—and the fact that only 0.7 percent of the overall force consists of management-level positions.[32]

ICITAP officials have identified five core areas in which they will assist Pakistan: (1) increasing border security; (2) facilitating law enforcement reform and training; (3) establishing an Automated Fingerprint Identification System (AFIS); (4) instituting a National Criminal Data Base (NCDB); and (5) building forensic capabilities.[33] In the short term, ICITAP will provide assistance in these areas to "help the Government of Pakistan develop an effective border control network that can respond effectively to various transnational criminal activities in a manner that is consistent with the highest professional standards, including internationally recognized human rights principles and the rule of law."[34] Over the longer term, ICITAP will try to work with other partner countries to further augment the professionalism of Pakistan's law enforcement agencies and eliminate corruption.

In addition to providing organizational and development consultations and technical assistance, ICITAP's collaborative initiatives will be aimed specifically at (1) enhancing interagency coordination and cooperation across Pakistan's various law enforcement agencies on issues related to border security; (2) providing management and leadership training to senior-level law enforcement officials; (3) delivering skills training to mid-level police and line officers; (4) augmenting investigative, training, and instructional capacities; and (5) facilitating police reform.[35]

The DEA

The bulk of DEA assistance to Pakistan is directed toward the country's Anti-Narcotics Task Force (ANF). Instituted as part of Operation Containment,[36] the DEA's efforts are aimed at stemming the flow of heroin from Afghanistan into Pakistan and has thus far involved the provision of new investigative resources, all-terrain vehicles, and surveillance motor-cycles.[37] In addition, the DEA has been instrumental in setting up at least one Special Investigative Unit (SIU) in Pakistan. The detachment, which is staffed by carefully vetted personnel trained and equipped to U.S. standards, has been instrumental in several significant seizures of opiates and arrests of traffickers.[38]

Areas of U.S. Assistance

State Penetration of the Border Areas and Enhanced Border Control

The INL has taken the lead in providing civilian security assistance in the border areas, with the main aim of helping Pakistan gain greater control of its 1,500-mile-long border with Afghanistan. In facilitating a more concerted state presence in the region, the INL hopes that Pakistani agencies will be able to more effectively counter terrorism and stem the illicit movement of persons, arms, narcotics, and smuggled goods. In FY04, the INL allocated some $26 million dollars to its various border-security efforts.[39]

Among the more important and widely advertised projects undertaken by the INL in Pakistan has been the introduction of a computerized Personal Identification Security, Comparison and Evaluation System (PISCES) to capture details about persons entering and exiting the country. In principal, the system is capable of mapping facial images against biometric data to verify an individual's identity and has the potential to be linked to similar FBI databases.[40] PISCES is now operational at all of the country's main airports, and there are plans to install additional components at key land-crossings at well.

The creation of an air wing in Quetta (in Baluchistan) is another highly visible project undertaken by the INL. The unit—officially known as a Forward Operating Base (FOB)—falls under the auspices of the MoI, which constitutes the INL's partner ministry in Pakistan. Since FY01, the United States has provided the air wing with three Caravan spotter planes, eight Huey II helicopters (which may be increased to ten over the next couple years), and ground support to keep these assets operational.[41] Washington's hope is that this assistance will provide Pakistan with a more robust capability to counter terrorism and engage in antinarcotics activities. This unit will also allow for more effective action in the areas of surveillance and reconnaissance, troop transport and rotation, logistical resupply, medical evacuation, and command and control.[42]

The INL has also been instrumental in expanding Pakistan's ground mobility capabilities through the provision of 1,100 border-security operations vehicles and critical surveillance equipment. Further, the INL has helped with the construction of several entry/exit checkpoints along the Pakistan-Afghanistan frontier and the establishment of border-security-intelligence coordination cells. It is also currently engaged in training Frontier Corps personnel, which, as noted, have primary responsibility in the tribal areas.[43]

As described in chapter 1, the frontier tribal areas lack significant lines of control and communication and other infrastructure that would facilitate the penetration of the state into these areas. With few roads in these areas, law enforcement agencies have encountered significant difficulties accessing them. Both the United States and Pakistan agree that much more infrastructure needs to be built to enable greater state penetration into these areas and to ensure that the state is able to exert control over them. Accordingly, an additional INL objective has focused on the laying of roads along the border. As of November 2004, 426 kilometers of roads had been built with an additional 391 kilometers under construction. The INL and the Pakistani government hoped that by the end of 2005 more than 50 percent of previously inaccessible areas would have become accessible through these efforts. (The authors are not in a position to determine whether this goal was met.)[44]

Certain S/CT and DS/ATA programs are also directed at enhancing Islamabad's ability to control its frontier with Afghanistan. The S/CT runs a class on border security that can be attended by personnel of various Pakistani security and police forces, including border patrol forces, the Frontier Constabulary, and any other force that is involved in these kinds of operations and is not active army.

Improving Pakistani Law Enforcement Capacity and Interagency Cooperation

The INL, along with its operational partner ICITAP, have instituted several programs aimed at reforming and modernizing law enforcement capabilities within Pakistan. Specifically, the INL is working to provide basic police training in the fundamentals of criminal investigation and crime-scene analysis and the principal of continuum of force. The bureau is also helping to develop organizational structures, leadership skills, and managerial abilities and is seeking to foster institutional values and accountability.[45]

While the vast majority of this work is undertaken by the INL, some key activities are complemented by programs instituted through ICITAP[46]— the main thrust of which are directed toward improving security forces' capabilities to detect and interdict illicit cross-border activities and the movement of illicit goods and narcotics.[47] Relevant training takes place in Quetta and Peshawar and involves the Frontier Constabulary, the ANF, customs and customs intelligence agencies, the Federal Investigative Agency (FIA), and immigration.[48]

ICITAP has also helped with institution building within Pakistan's national police force[49] and provides in-country assistance to support INL's Border Security Project and related police-reform activities through the provision of technical assistance, equipment donation, and training resources.[50] Further, various external instructional courses have been offered in the United States, including modules on border-security[51] augmentation, crime-scene investigation, first response procedures,[52] and senior management duties.[53] Further, ICITAP has worked on improving Pakistan's highly rudimentary forensics capabilities, particularly in terms of furnishing the country's existing four laboratories[54] with the means to undertake essential operations, such as the testing and comparing of blood samples and ballistics.[55] ICITAP had hoped to work with Pakistan on establishing a true national forensics infrastructure. However, for reasons to be discussed in the next chapter, this effort has not yet come to fruition.[56]

Additionally, ICITAP has been particularly active—together with the S/CT and the INL—in the creation of the AFIS and the NCDB.

AFIS

U.S. officials highlight two main reasons for helping Pakistan establish an AFIS: (1) to provide the police with an important investigative tool and (2) to help Pakistan in quickly identifying terrorists.[57]

Pakistan's AFIS is currently in its first stage of development. This phase involves U.S. experts and officials working with their Pakistani counterparts to draw up strategies for establishing a central mainframe computer within the FIA, for operationalizing networked multifunctional workstations in the country's four provinces,[58] for allowing officials in these provinces to access the data housed at FIA, and for instituting remote terminals in fifty of Pakistan's 107 districts.[59] The second stage will focus on installing remote terminals in those districts not covered in the first phase. Each district will be provided with a computer, a scanner for fingerprint cards, a trained operator, and network connectivity.[60]

NCDB

The NCDB is the second major Pakistani law enforcement program under development with U.S. assistance. Originally, the AFIS and the NCDB were to be developed as a combined effort. However, for a number of reasons, this proved unfeasible and the projects were split apart at the request of the secretary of the MoI, which felt that the AFIS needed to be established first. Unfortunately, there has been little movement on the NCDB to date. This is due to a variety of problems that will be addressed in chapter 3.

ICITAP personnel estimate that the NCDB, even with its modest objectives, will cost some $4 million to create.[61] Notably, DNA analysis is *not* part of the basic capabilities being developed by ICITAP. ICITAP officials state that Pakistan currently lacks the fundamental human capital inputs needed to sustain a DNA-analytic program, noting that building basic forensic analytic programs in countries that do have trained technicians is challenging enough. They further maintain that even if the U.S. and its international partners trained Pakistani technicians in the ways of DNA analysis, by the time a relevant national lab came on-line, the technology would have already changed so much as to make this initial training redundant.[62] That said, one high-ranking member of the Pakistani police informed the authors that while the U.S. initiative has yet to materialize, China has committed to providing both training facilities and equipment for the creation of a DNA lab. This same official also asserted that the Japanese government is prepared to fund teaching modules for twelve Pakistanis in Japan, with the idea that they will then provide DNA education to Pakistani technicians on returning home.[63]

Counternarcotics Programming

For FY04, the United States allocated $10.8 million to strengthen Pakistan's narcotics law enforcement. This aid, channeled through the INL, was designed to (1) help Pakistan interdict drugs smugglers through an enhanced security presence on the Pakistan-Afghanistan border and (2) provide a means for eradicating residual poppy cultivation in the NWFP and Baluchistan. Central activities in support of these efforts include building access and "farm-to-market" roads in previously inaccessible frontier areas; encouraging the planting of alternative crops; assisting with the spraying of crops; and fostering small-scale development projects. These initiatives have been especially prominent in the Bajaur, Mohmand, and Khyber agencies of FATA.[64]

The INL also funds Narcotics Coordination Cells in both the Home Department of the NWFP and the FATA Secretariat with the hope that these cells will assist with the coordination of counternarcotics efforts in the tribal areas. In addition, the DEA has provided commodity assistance to fortify the ANF and, as noted, has been instrumental in setting up at least one dedicated SIU for antidrug purposes.

Human Trafficking

While many of the above-noted programs focus broadly on border security and counternarcotics efforts, a few U.S.-financed initiatives specifically address human trafficking,[65] focusing on prevention, protection, and prosecution.[66] Provided through the International Organization for Migration (IOM), the $103,800 earmarked for these efforts in FY04 allowed the organization to launch Pakistan's first ever countertrafficking training module for senior law enforcement personnel. The course was well attended by the FIA, which is currently the main agency in Pakistan responsible for fighting the human trade.[67] Overall, however, Washington's assistance to Pakistan in this area has been marginal. In FY04, for instance, the United States funded 271 countertrafficking programs worldwide, seventeen of which were in South Asia. Of these, only one was sponsored in Pakistan.[68] While there is no publicly available information to explain this lack of attention, it may reflect the fact that the Pakistani government has yet to implement needed legislation for combating human trafficking.[69]

Terrorism Financing

U.S. officials note that all South Asian countries need to improve their antiterrorist financing regimes. However, they single out Pakistan as a state of particular priority on account of the internal presence of al-Qaeda and other foreign jihadist groups, the country's notoriously porous border areas, and the continued persistence of a thriving informal cash-based *hawala* economy that extends beyond Pakistan and throughout the region.[70]

Several U.S. law enforcement and regulatory agencies have provided limited training and technical assistance to Pakistan on how to undertake money-laundering countermeasures and financial investigations. U.S. officials are eager to expand this support and also want to work with Pakistan in other important areas as well, such as in preventing criminals and terrorists from exploiting the nonprofit sector and helping with the creation of a Financial Intelligence Unit (FIU).[71] However, while the Musharraf government has taken initiatives to regulate *hawala* channels and freeze certain al-Qaeda assets, it has yet to pass comprehensive antiterrorist financing legislation that meets international standards.[72] Until this occurs, moves within the United States to provide more concerted support to Pakistan on the antiterrorist financing front will have to remain, as one State Department official put it, "on the back burner."[73]

Corruption and Governance

Under USAID's current five-year strategic plan (2003–07), some $64.5 million will be allocated to improve Pakistan's democratic institutions and practices.[74] While the planned USAID initiatives are important, they do not explicitly address the kinds of problems and threats identified in chapter 1. For instance, the USAID program on Democracy and Good Governance will simply focus on "fostering new leadership within issue-based civil society organizations and political parties; fostering the creation of new fora in which civil society, political leaders, and local civil administration authorities can discuss and reach consensus on priority development issues; and improving the capacity to carry out research and analyses designed to inform decision-makers, lawmakers and civil society leaders on the state of political change in Pakistan."[75]

USAID—along with other international partners—is also involved in financing Transparency International–Pakistan (TI-P).[76] Officially recognized in February 2001, TI-P was one of USAID's numerous grantees in FY04, receiving funding to expand and improve the capacity of national and provincial legislators and legislatures.[77] However, in this instance, too, USAID is not providing the type of support needed for aggressively addressing the types of threats identified in chapter 1.[78]

Conclusions

Current U.S. assistance to Pakistan is focused heavily through the lens of the GWOT. Washington concentrates the bulk of its resources on the Pakistan-Afghanistan frontier, targeting activities that either appear to originate there or are particularly intense in that region. Accordingly, U.S. efforts to enhance the capabilities of Islamabad's varied law enforcement agencies have a strong bias to those bodies with mandated responsibilities for the border areas. The calculus for this emphasis on FATA likely rests on the assumption that such support is the most effective way of bolstering Pakistan's internal security environment and ensuring that it does not provide a conducive theater for jihadist extremism and related threats to transnational security. Overall, however, significant gaps remain in U.S. assistance coverage. For example, although there are looming threats in the country's interior, relatively few resources have been made available to deal directly with problems there. Further, even though Pakistan is beset by endemic corruption, an ineffective judiciary, and extensive drugs smuggling and human trafficking, Washington has paid only marginal attention to ameliorating these particular challenges—despite their proven negative impact on the viability of the Pakistani state. The significance of these assistance shortcomings to Pakistani and U.S. interests and ways to address them will be discussed in the final chapter.

3

Assessment of U.S. Law Enforcement Assistance to Pakistan

The general consensus among U.S. and Pakistani officials interviewed for this study is that the current regime of U.S. law enforcement assistance to Pakistan is relevant to Islamabad's needs and is playing an important role in helping the government address some of the more glaring deficiencies in its domestic security arrangements. PISCES, AFIS, the air wing within MoI, and the SIG have all been hailed as particularly useful, providing both the foundation for a far more robust regime of frontier control and the means to undertake decisive antiterrorist initiatives and related criminal investigations.[1] That said, the true potential of U.S. assistance has been limited both by shortcomings in Pakistan and by the specific way in which programs have been developed and initiated by Washington. To cast light on these various limitations and to find ways of optimizing the U.S. assistance programs to Pakistan, this final chapter brings together multifarious insights gained from discussions with interlocutors in both Pakistan and the United States.

Overview of Threats and U.S. Assistance Programs to Pakistan

Pakistan's threat environment and the slate of U.S. internal security assistance programs to Pakistan were discussed in chapters 1 and 2. The question now is: how well do these specific programs address the threats?

Jihadist Terrorism

U.S. efforts to help Pakistan contend with the threat from jihadist terrorism are most apparent in those activities aimed at preventing foreign militant infiltration into Pakistan's northern and western frontier and border areas, as well as militant exfiltration from these parts of Pakistan into Afghanistan. While the United States has offered comparatively few resources to support counterterrorism efforts outside this zone of concern, it has initiated several programs to augment the capability of Islamabad's civilian security agencies. Ultimately, however, Pakistan's will to permanently move away from using Islamist militancy as an instrument of foreign policy will be of even greater importance for domestic stability and security than the magnitude of U.S. civilian security assistance to the country.

Sectarian Violence

Sectarian violence within Pakistan is an important issue but one that remains largely beyond the purview of U.S. assistance programs. State Department officials see this particular threat essentially as a domestic issue that is best addressed through general efforts to strengthen Pakistan's internal security architecture.[2] The potential links between Sunni sectarian organizations, such as LeJ, and other internal and external Islamist entities, such as JeM, LeT, and al-Qaeda, do not appear to have yet factored into Washington's thinking.

Narcotics Traffic

The United States—along with Great Britain and other close allies—is actively involved in a number of programs that directly address narcotics trafficking in Pakistan.

Organized Crime

There is no direct U.S. assistance program to counter the threat posed by organized crime in Pakistan. As with sectarian violence, the United States regards this issue as one that can be dealt with as a "by-product" of other INL programs.

Smuggling of Goods and Trafficking of People

While the United States has initiated a number of programs that are directly and indirectly intended to help Pakistan contain the smuggling of goods (e.g., through efforts on the Pakistan-Afghanistan border), the United States has done little to help the country deal with human trafficking. This is due—at least in part—to Pakistan's own historical reticence to acknowledge the problem. The Musharraf government itself has only recently begun to regard human trade as a serious issue.

Table 6. U.S. Security Assistance and the Extant Pakistani Internal Threat Environment

Identified Threat	U.S. Programs Designed to Address Threat	Remarks
Jihadist Terrorism	Various INL and ICITAP programs to address foreign militants in FATA; Initiatives to increase capabilities of law enforcement agencies	Few efforts to direct counterterror resources outside the tribal area belt
Sectarian Violence	No specific programs	The United States considers this to be a domestic issue that can be addressed under general efforts to enhance Pakistan's internal security architecture.
Drugs Trafficking	Numerous INL and DEA programs	
Organized Crime	No specific programs	The United States considers organized crime as an issue that can be addressed as a "by-product" of other INL programs.
Smuggling of Goods and Trafficking in People	Several INL programs aimed at countering smuggling of goods across the Pakistan-Afghanistan border	No direct programs to counter trafficking in persons
Corruption and Governance	Limited USAID educational initiatives in FATA	Resources not dedicated to the wider provision of justice, democracy, and bureaucratic accountability

Source: Summary of findings from chapters 1 and 2 of this study

Corruption and Poor Governance

Although the United States has identified corruption and poor governance in Pakistan as serious sources of instability, U.S. programs currently do not address the core problems related to both that were highlighted in chapter 1. For example, most of USAID's activities revolve around increasing educational initiatives in the tribal border areas and not around promoting wider objectives pertaining to justice, democracy, and bureaucratic accountability.

In this post-9/11 era, the United States has expressed deep satisfaction with the positive actions that Pakistan has taken in addressing several areas of security concern, some of which are especially sensitive for Islamabad, such as the proscription of Islamist groups and NGOs that the United States has designated as foreign terrorist organizations (FTO). As evidence of the Musharraf government's proactive attitude toward addressing such concerns, one State Department official pointed to Islamabad's closure of al Haramain's Pakistani office, an action undertaken before the al-Qaeda-linked charity was designated as an FTO by the United States.[3]

U.S. officials have also praised Pakistan's ability to quickly institute creative solutions to improve the performance of assistance programs. For instance, when PISCES first came on-line in Pakistan's major airports, its implementation was severely constrained by an overwhelmingly male-oriented staff that was largely corrupt and unable to rapidly master the fundamentals of the new system. In response, Islamabad recruited and trained an alternate cadre of young female immigration officers, who proved to be more adroit in data management techniques and who were not tainted by the corrupt practices of many of their older predecessors.[4] At present, PISCES is performing smoothly at virtually all of Pakistan's principal immigration points and is being run by both male and female officers.[5]

Just as important, Pakistan has affirmed the bulk of Washington's support as valuable and pertinent to the country's internal security needs. In commenting on the utility of the overall U.S. security package, Akhatar Munir Marawat, the joint secretary of the MoI, remarked: "U.S. assistance has been channeled to the appropriate places and reflects the priorities of the government."[6] While U.S. and Pakistani interlocutors generally concur that this recent U.S.-Pakistan engagement has been beneficial and productive, several significant problems and deficiencies remain in the current assistance package. If these various shortcomings could in some measure be remedied, potentially even greater returns on investment could be realized. Enhancing the efficacy of extant programs would not only serve the interests of both the United States and Pakistan but would also have a salutary effect upon the stability of the wider South Asian region.

Shortcomings Specific to Pakistan's Contribution to the Bilateral Security Engagement

Pakistan has been unable to effectively absorb U.S. security assistance or otherwise institute a rigorous structure of law enforcement and criminal justice. These shortcomings are associated with (1) institutional challenges within Pakistan's domestic police and intelligence agencies; (2) the questionable willingness and/or ability of Islamabad to comprehensively crackdown on Islamist militants operating in the country; and (3) complicating legislative frameworks.

Institutional Challenges within Domestic Police and Intelligence Agencies

U.S. officials highlight a number of institutional challenges within Pakistan's domestic police and intelligence setup that dramatically complicate the core mission of law enforcement reform and capacity-building in Pakistan. First, the country's various security agencies are "stovepiped," remaining devoid of any meaningful sense of horizontal integration—both in terms of information sharing and functional working or logistical partnerships. Existing problems have been significantly exacerbated by the fact that many organizations have overlapping and poorly delineated responsibilities. Further, there are a lack of effective bureaucratic mechanisms within Pakistan for quickly and efficiently convening joint operational taskforces to deal with threats that cross jurisdictional boundaries and mandates. Curiously, the JWG-CTLE has come to serve as an important interagency process for Pakistan in the absence of other such structures.[7]

Second, the manner by which Pakistani participants are chosen for training programs is frequently not based on merit or competence. State Department officials lament that often the right people are not sent to appropriate instructional courses held in the United States, observing there is a tendency to pick the highest-ranking police official for such training or to "provide a vacation option to the deserving." Such practices do little to maximize the return of investment in U.S.-based training programs or to ensure the efficacious duplication of course modules in Pakistan. U.S. officials would prefer that Pakistan send officials who are recognized as the best trainer or instructor and who are, thus, in a better position to impart what they have learned to police cadres "at home."[8] To address this problem, Washington should examine how other allied donor countries—such as Great Britain—accredit personnel for their law enforcement programs. Washington should then, together with those countries, formulate a comprehensive schematic that can be used both to vet Pakistani applicants before they are sent for overseas training and—just as crucially—to audit their performance after they return home.

Third, several U.S. officials remarked that Pakistan is not particularly adroit at exploiting the utility of "stand-alone" courses offered to its law enforcement personnel. Officers that are dispatched to attend modules on bomb disposal, for instance, may well be reassigned to an area—such as traffic control—that has little, if any, relevance to the training that was provided. These types of postcourse deployments are highly problematic, as the individuals in question have no opportunity to maintain the acquired skills or to impart the acquired knowledge to others.[9]

Fourth, statutory problems have prevented the comprehensive implementation of certain assistance programs. This has been most evident in efforts to establish a rigorous regime for countering terrorist financing. Although the United States has singled out Pakistan as a high-priority country for receiving assistance in this area, very little progress has been made in actually instituting key schematic initiatives to combat terrorist financing, such as creating a dedicated FIU.[10] This seems to imply a lack of political will in Islamabad, which is further suggested by the fact that Pakistan has neither signed the UN Convention for the Suppression of the Financing of Terrorism nor passed an adequate suite of fiscal legislation that meets international standards. U.S. interlocutors explain that this apparent lack of will on Pakistan's part is not due to a desire to protect terrorist financing channels; rather, it relates to the political difficulty of closing down channels that have been lucrative for politicians and other influential persons. Regardless of the causes of this unwillingness, the United States will not provide additional support in this area until Islamabad puts into place the appropriate legislative framework.[11]

Fifth, pervasive corruption throughout Pakistan has put limits on the kinds of programs that Washington can initialize with Islamabad. For example, according to officials in both countries, the Musharraf government is actively soliciting assistance to fortify security in Karachi's port. However, the United States has, thus far, been unwilling to support such an effort, arguing that there would be little value in providing Pakistan with the technical means to secure the port and its containers without first rooting out the endemic corruption that is widely acknowledged to be undermining the integrity of the coastal city's warehouse-to-port supply chain. Unfortunately, the United States has few means of determining whether Islamabad has substantively dealt with the corruption issue, a necessary precondition for participating in container-security programs. For the time being, therefore, such programs will not likely be instituted in Karachi.[12]

Sixth, various compensatory, organizational, and geographic problems impact on the overall efficacy of Pakistan's law enforcement structure. U.S. Justice Department officials note that Pakistani officers, due to being severely underpaid, remain "susceptible to outside influences and corruption, and are not respected by the public."[13] These officials similarly deride the police's critically low functional investigative ratio and the paucity of manager-level positions. Additionally, the topography of Pakistan's western border areas, together with the dearth of roads and other infrastructure in FATA and the region's tenacious support for al-Qaeda and Taliban elements, have combined to dramatically complicate the ability of existing law enforcement organizations to fulfill effectively their statutory mandates.[14]

Pakistan's Willingness and/or Ability to Comprehensively Crack Down on Islamist Militants

Pakistan continues to confront serious threats from jihadist and sectarian groups. These challenges will persist regardless of the level of U.S. assistance to the Musharraf government, as they relate more directly to the decisions taken by the Pakistani government itself. It is widely believed in Washington and elsewhere that many of the threats to Pakistan are strongly correlated to the country's own long-standing policy of supporting jihadist *tanzeems* to prosecute foreign policy objectives in Kashmir, India, and Afghanistan. Not surprisingly, Islamabad strongly rejects this line of argument. While acknowledging the past existence of actively militant Kashmir and Afghanistan policies, Pakistan stresses that such policies are now defunct. As proof of this, Pakistani officials point to the country's abandonment of the Taliban in 2001 and the proscription of the LeT, HuM, and JeM in 2002.[15]

U.S.—and certain Pakistani—commentators take such Pakistani assertions with a grain of salt, observing that banned organizations within Pakistan are frequently allowed to resurface under different names, that many
arrested jihadist leaders are eventually released on questionable legal
grounds,[16] and that stated attempts to more closely regulate extremist
madaris (however small in number) have, thus far, yielded few results.[17]
A number of U.S. officials also suggest the possibility that Pakistan may be
deliberately harboring Pakhtun militants as a conduit through which to
project Pakistani influence into the nascent post-Taliban Afghan state.[18]

Additionally, Pakistan identifies militants as either sectarian domestic
terrorists or mujahadeen fighting for the liberation of Kashmir;[19] the latter
are explicitly portrayed and exonerated as "freedom fighters" to be promoted and defended in their (fully legitimate) efforts to wrest the disputed
province from India, while the former are uniformly denigrated as criminals to be rooted out, arrested, or otherwise eliminated. Making such distinctions is highly problematic and has direct implications on the stability
of the state. As discussed in chapter 1, there is strong evidence to suggest
that Sunni sectarian groups such as the SSP and LeJ share an overlapping
membership with the Kashmiri-oriented JeM. These groups also emerge
from the same religious interpretative school (Deobandism) and have several important *madaris* in common. More disturbing is the fact that both
the JeM and LeJ are thought to maintain links with the al-Qaeda network.
Further, since 9/11, they have engaged in joint operations against the
Musharraf government and foreign interests in Pakistan, such as in the
2002 attack on French engineers in Karachi.[20] In short, efforts to differentiate sectarian violence from Kashmiri—or, indeed, imported—jihadism
may not only be overly simplistic but also fundamentally at odds with
evolving realities on the ground.

Musharraf's political opponents repeatedly highlight the current
regime's inability to rid the country of religious extremism and to institu-
tionalize the often-enunciated vision of a stable and progressive Pakistan as
enshrined in the concept of "enlightened moderation." These critics
charge this failure is attributable to a lack of sincerity and willingness on the
part of the government to make a strategic move to abandon the use of
militancy in prosecuting its foreign policy objectives. Other observers,
meanwhile, including numerous foreign diplomats in Pakistan, believe that

the continuing Islamist threat has more to do with the government's inca-
pacity to understand the enormity of the problem and its inability to act
accordingly.[21] Whatever the truth of the matter, all efforts to restore internal stability to Pakistan will not fully fructify until Pakistan makes a visible
and unambiguous commitment to permanently cease support for jihadists
of all kinds.[22]

Complicating Legislative Frameworks

A number of problems relating to Pakistan's legislative framework have
surfaced in recent years, at least two of which have adversely affected wider
efforts aimed at police reform within the existing force structure. The first
legislative framework problem affects the work of the SIG, which ICITAP
helped to establish within the FIA. The original idea was that SIG officers
would be invested with skills comparable to that of an FBI counterpart.
Although the agency now has thirty-seven full-time investigators, they
have no ability to pursue cases beyond the federal territory of Islamabad,
as legal protocols have yet to be developed to assign specific and separate
jurisdictional authority outside this area. As long as this situation prevails,
the SIG will not be able to evolve into what could be a meaningful and
important *national* investigative force that is able to contribute to cases in
Pakistan's enormous cities, such as Lahore and Karachi, or in other locali-
ties within the country's four provinces.[23]

A second and, arguably, even more problematic issue relating to Pakistan's legislative framework involves the Police Order (PO) of 2002,[24]
which was meant to reform Pakistan's law enforcement structure. When
first constituted, the police ordinance was deemed highly progressive; it
not only included a number of important oversight and accountability
mechanisms—such as a citizen's complaint board—to review cases of
alleged police abuse, but it also aimed to minimize political interference by
instituting a transparent and robust system for determining individual promotions and geographic assignments.[25] However, this particular piece of
legislation was never made into law, and in 2004, the Federal Parliament
passed a greatly revised version of the 2002 order, which includes a statutory provision that makes the police accountable to the lowest level of
elected officialdom—the *nazim*.[26]

The Musharraf government has supported the new PO of 2004 on two interrelated grounds. First, the revised order links police reform to President Musharraf's general policy of devolving central government power to the periphery, a move that the United States supports.[27] Second, in stressing the role of the *nazim*, the order makes the police more accountable to local elected bodies, which, at least in theory, are supposed to be independent and free of party influence.[28]

However, opponents of the new PO question the sincerity of Musharraf's devolution agenda, arguing that it is simply designed to entrench the military's dominance over civilian affairs by further marginalizing Pakistan's embattled mainstream political parties—the Pakistan's Peoples Party (PPP), led by Benazir Bhutto, and the Pakistan Muslim League, (PML), led by Nawaz Sharif.[29] Further, opponents express deep ambivalence over placing law enforcement under the purview of the *nazim*. They argue that this will, in fact, make it *more* difficult for police to operate on behalf of the citizens and will provide even greater incentive for officers to function as the personal thugs of local politicians.[30]

This ongoing debate is relevant to how much of an impact U.S. law enforcement assistance will have on Pakistan. While Washington's assistance is not likely to have direct nefarious consequences for human rights, there is little prospect that this assistance will generate a meaningful return on investment if Pakistan is not fully committed to enacting a concerted and genuine reform process of its own. U.S. assistance in itself will likely only have a marginal effect—if any—in eliciting a more professional and effective policing structure truly responsive and answerable to the civilian needs of the country.

Problems Associated with the U.S. Provision of Security Assistance

A number of problems exist with respect to the manner in which the United States has provided security assistance to Pakistan. These problems relate to the focus, formulation and assessment, structural initialization, and general prioritization and coverage of the assistance programs.

The Singular Focus on Musharraf and the Pakistan Army Rather Than on Civil Society

One key problem with the U.S. internal security programs in Pakistan lies not so much in their specific institution but in the overall framework of U.S. engagement with Pakistan. As noted in chapter 2, a considerable proportion of Washington's support takes the form of FMF, the main aim of which is to secure the tenure of President Musharraf by placating his primary stakeholder—the military. Such an approach is viewed by the United States as critical both in shoring up an important ally in the GWOT and in preventing a radical destabilization of the world's only nuclear-armed Islamic state.[31]

Despite the salience of these considerations, the singular focus of the United States on Musharraf and the armed forces carries direct implications for Pakistan's civilian governance and law and order. The overwhelming bias toward consolidating the power and position of the military is likely to have deleterious long-term effects on the country's *civil* society and ability to develop robust processes of democracy, good governance, and human rights.[32] The support Pakistan's army and security forces have given to militants operating in J&K testifies to the questionable wisdom of directly supporting a military regime. Pakistan's use of irregular fighters to resolve the Kashmir dispute has been a major contributing factor in the human rights crisis that has persisted in the disputed region since 1989. (To be sure, the Indian armed forces and numerous other armed militant organizations fighting in the region are also deeply culpable in this crisis.)[33] Democracy advocates maintain that these activities alone should prompt some reflection about the way in which the United States currently governs its relationship with Pakistan and the manner by which it allocates its security assistance to the central government.[34]

Within Pakistan, meanwhile, there is a palpable fear among some that the United States will retreat from the country once its interest in combating terrorism in South Asia wanes. The main concern is that should this occur, Washington's aid will have been instrumental in consolidating the power of an unelected military regime and will have had no meaningful impact on the fostering of viable democratic institutions. In fact, civil rights commentators contend that the Pakistani government has tried to exploit the U.S. abandonment theme for its own ends by imparting feelings of guilt on U.S. officials to garner—often successfully—even more immediate and substantive assistance for the armed forces.[35] The United States would be wise to not discount these fears, however—particularly in light of a 2005 Pew Research Center poll that found that less than 23 percent of urban Pakistanis were favorably inclined to the evolving nature of U.S. foreign policy in the post-9/11 era.[36]

The Near Exclusive Bias toward Hard Security

The bulk of U.S. assistance to Pakistan has largely been unidimensional in nature, mostly emphasizing hard security while paying scant regard to wider—and just as critical—civic outreach programs, such as those designed to ameliorate underlying drivers of Islamist extremism. USAID's burgeoning effort to address poverty, unemployment, and other socio-economic conditions in FATA that contribute to popular malaise, alienation, and frustration is a notable exception to this.[37] However, modalities for establishing robust structures of community-based policing—which are vital to the institution of any effective system of local law enforcement—have yet to feature prominently within current U.S. assistance programs to Pakistan.[38]

Geographic Concentration on the Tribal and Border Areas

In terms of geopolitical focus, the Bush administration has tended to anchor the majority of its counterterrorism assistance on enhancing border security along Pakistan's northern and western frontiers with Afghanistan. Although this region is undoubtedly an important point of infiltration for al-Qaeda and Taliban militants, it is not the only zone of concern. Indeed, as noted earlier, Pakistani intelligence officials—who arguably have the most complete understanding of the current workings of jihadist networks in South Asia—state that since the army's 2004 incursions into South Waziristan, the crux of the jihadist presence has steadily shifted to the country's hinterlands and to major cities such as Quetta, Lahore, and especially Karachi. However, the direction of Washington's counter-terrorism assistance has not kept pace with these developments. A case in point is the MoI's highly publicized air wing. Under the U.S.-prepared terms of reference for its use, aerial assets are restricted to carrying out reconnaissance duties solely within the vicinity of the tribal and border areas,[39] which already have a substantial security force presence. As several officials in the MoI pointed out, the unit would be far better employed assisting with surveillance along the Makran coast and the remote interiors of Baluchistan—where 95 percent of the territory does not have a police presence—and Sindh.[40]

Programmatic Implementation and Assessment

The United States retains a very thin presence in Pakistan. Outside of the capital, Washington has very few "on-ground" assets, especially in Karachi where there are frequent specific threats to Westerners. Therefore, the monitoring of assistance programs—particularly in terms of verifying that money is spent as intended and that provided goods and services are utilized as specified—has proven to be extremely difficult. Although INL officials stationed at the U.S. embassy in Islamabad are highly keen to venture into the country to better assess the situation, they are frequently prevented from doing so because of the security environment and generally are allowed to travel only to areas where forward-operating bases—such as the one in Quetta—have been established.[41] This situation effectively prevents the United States from determining whether real progress has been made or whether significant retrenchment from reform is taking place. The previously discussed problems pertaining to corruption and container security in Karachi underscore this dilemma.[42]

Structural Impediments to Effective Implementation

A number of structural impediments within Pakistan currently impair the effective implementation of U.S. assistance efforts. Language is a major barrier and one that has had direct effects on many of the training programs currently being run in-country. Several U.S. officials have noted that in their experience, Pakistani participants are frequently illiterate or not thoroughly proficient in English. By the same token, the United States has only a limited number of Urdu speakers that it can call on and even fewer who are conversant in Punjabi, Sindhi, Baluch, or Pashto. Difficulties have consequently arisen in terms of expeditiously imparting and receiving knowledge and ensuring that instructional courses achieve their primary aims.[43]

Another structural problem relates to the manner in which some equipment is provided to Pakistan. Most of the assets supplied to the MoI air wing, for instance, are technically provided on loan, which allows the United States to directly monitor and control the way these products are employed. While required by the terms of the lease from the U.S. government, this arrangement has produced some degree of ill will among Pakistanis, who feel that it is an infringement on their country's national sovereignty and freedom of action. Such perceptions are especially marked when U.S. officials demand to see flight logs to verify that the air wing's helicopters have only been used for reconnaissance and surveillance duties in the tribal and border areas. Many pilots have been taken aback by these requests, arguing that they reflect a lack of trust on the part of the United States and underscore a bilateral relationship between Washington and Islamabad that is somewhat akin to that of a father and son.[44]

Tentative Recommendations

As this chapter has highlighted, the true potential of U.S. backing to Pakistan is being hindered by limitations in the country's intent and its absorptive capacity and by implementation problems related to the actual institution of the U.S. assistance package—in terms of both coverage and wider considerations of good governance and human rights. The United States certainly cannot be expected to shoulder the burden of reforming Islamabad's internal security structure on its own, but it can do more to strengthen civilian law enforcement in Pakistan by considering the following recommendations.

Bolster Pakistan's Will to Do More

The interests of the Pakistani state itself sometimes clash with the objectives of comprehensive law and order reform and/or the interests of the United States and the wider global community. The state's support for Islamist militants based in the country is one such manifestation of this fact. It is very unlikely that international assistance to Pakistan will have a long-term palliative effect unless Islamabad makes a strategic decision to fully abandon militancy as a means of prosecuting its foreign and security policy. Islamabad's current attempt to differentiate between al-Qaeda, components of the Taliban, and domestic jihadist groups is a grave mistake; many of these groups are integrated at the level of membership and ideology, share the same mosques and *madaris*, and continue to enjoy at least some measure of ISI support.

Unfortunately, given its preoccupation with the GWOT, the Bush administration has done little—at least publicly—to address Pakistan's propensity for making such inutile distinctions. The United States and international community must give this issue the prioritization that it deserves. This may mean leaning on New Delhi and Kabul, inter alia, to foster conditions that will cause Pakistan to reassess its belief that Islamist proxies are needed to prosecute its foreign policy objectives in India and Afghanistan. For example, the United States should impress upon Kabul that it cannot expect Pakistan to *respect* the sanctity of the Durand line separating the two states when Kabul itself does not even *recognize* the Durand line as a *de facto*—much less as a *de jure*—border. Similarly, India needs to see the value of *resolving* its territorial dispute with Pakistan over the Line of Control separating Indian- and Pakistan-administered portions of Kashmir. The United States should fully exploit the fact that it has unprecedented relations with these three states, whose internal and external security policies are deeply intertwined, to find regional solutions for these interrelated policy puzzles. To ensure Pakistan's cooperation in such processes, a number of prominent South Asia analysts have further suggested that the provision of certain aspects of military aid should be made contingent on Pakistan meeting significant benchmarks in cracking down on all forms of militancy in the country.[45]

Comprehensive progress on other complex issues, such as police reform, devolution, and the institution of a robust system of civil democracy, has been just as halting. Many of Pakistan's difficulties in these areas stem from the government's own policies and preferences for the country's inherited political structure. For this reason, "top-down" efforts at change may never fully fructify or filter down through the inner institutional workings of the state. This suggests that the United States should work more closely with Pakistani civil-society groups and NGOs to promote good governance at the grassroots level, emphasizing such tools and mechanisms as neighborhood action committees and even dedicated public service announcements. Washington needs to pay far closer attention to these wider "domestic concerns," not least because the direction they ultimately take will directly impinge upon the overall efficacy of U.S. assistance investments and support programs.

Strengthen and Broaden U.S. Anti-narcotics Programming

Pakistani agencies and officials question certain aspects of U.S. counternarcotics programs.[46] First, ANF officials are concerned about the funding tradeoffs inherent in Washington's sizeable near-term counternarcotics assistance to Afghanistan. They note, with considerable merit, that the nascent government in Kabul simply does not possess the necessary national infrastructure to effectively absorb this support. They contend this is deeply problematic given the unprecedented volume of poppies being cultivated inside Afghanistan and the concomitant need to strengthen the interdiction capabilities of the six Asian containment states critical to limiting the dispersion of the crop. They fear that the current direction of U.S. funding priorities will deprive these key states of the aid needed to counter the flow of drugs from South Asia.[47]

Second, ANF officials also assert that U.S. policies are largely based on a simplistic, monocausal interpretation of the drug problem; namely, that success is merely contingent on interdiction and curtailing supply in source countries. They are particularly concerned about the lack of initiatives to deal with the demand for narcotics in Pakistan, pointing out that funding for measures such as addict rehabilitation services, safe-needle exchanges, and public educational outreach programs remain at marginal levels. ANF officials believe these areas are critical for comprehensively dealing with the country's drug problem and burgeoning HIV/AIDS crisis.[48] While decreasing the demand for illicit drugs in Pakistan will not likely have a decisive impact on stemming the overall flow of opiates from Afghanistan, it will foster a more stable internal environment in the country. In turn, this will allow the government to play a more effective role in regional counternarcotics drives.

Third, the Frontier Corps has expressed consternation that it is not receiving support commensurate with its status as the only force in the immediate vicinity of the Afghanistan-FATA border area currently able to address internal law and order and trafficking problems.[49] While Pakistani agencies have a vested interest in arguing that they are not receiving adequate funding and assistance—indeed, U.S. officials based in Islamabad have even raised significant questions about the ANF's utilization of the resources it has received[50]—the concerns highlighted above are important and should be taken seriously.

Focus More Resources upon Organized Crime, Human Trafficking, Corruption, and Good Governance

The current U.S. internal security package does not specifically address a number of different threats to the overall stability of Pakistan, such as those related to organized crime, human trafficking, and the lack of viable civil governance structures. The United States, therefore, should consider expanding its programs to address these important sources of insecurity. For example, USAID could work directly with T I and other like organizations to address these and related concerns. Similarly, targeted law enforcement programs could provide the niche expertise needed to effectively counter criminal activities that threaten the state's stability.

Encourage Pakistan to Take Concerted Action against Jihadist and Sectarian Violence

U.S. officials have been hesitant to publicly encourage Pakistan to take more direct action against extremist violence and have also been reluctant to point out the obvious linkage between sectarian groups and other militant organizations—even al-Qaeda. However, a high-level diplomatic discourse should be initiated between the United States and Pakistan to impress upon Islamabad that militant Islamist extremism must be seen in its totality and that all of its various dimensions must be recognized as a direct threat not only to U.S. interests but also to Pakistan itself.

Areas beyond FATA

The United States should significantly reconsider the overwhelming emphasis it is currently giving to FATA in terms of internal security assistance. While this focus is undoubtedly important for the conduct of U.S. and coalition military operations in Afghanistan, it gives short shrift to the myriad and growing domestic law and order challenges that exist beyond the tribal border region. Notable areas of neglect include Pakistan's major urban conglomerations—where the vast majority of high-level al-Qaeda operatives have been caught—the country's ports, and the thickly forested areas of Sindh, NWFP, Azad Kashmir, and Punjab.

Conclusion

Most South Asia observers understand that just as Pakistan's current internal situation has taken decades to evolve, so too will it likely take considerable time for the state to emerge as a fully democratic entity that respects human rights and provides both security and good governance for its citizens. It is probably less well appreciated, however, that present U.S. interventions to support the state, while instrumental in the short-term GWOT, may seriously impede the long-term prospects for peace and stability in the country. Washington's actions in the region during the 1980s provide ample evidence of the necrotic effects such tradeoffs can have on wider social, political, and military growth. One of the prime challenges for the United States, therefore, is to determine how best to use its resources in a manner that is not only expeditious today but also consistent with the goal of shaping a viable and effective polity in Pakistan tomorrow. Critically, to what extent is the current suite of assistance being offered to President Musharraf and the army negatively impacting other aspects of Pakistan's social and political development?

The United States has a major stake in ensuring it formulates an assistance package that appropriately balances immediate security concerns with more latent considerations of open and responsible government. This is not only vital to enriching the lives of some 150 million Pakistanis who deserve to live under a solid democratic system, but it is also integral—for the following three reasons—to the stability of the greater South Asian region and the world.

First, the fate of Afghanistan is intrinsically linked to that of Pakistan: policies aimed at stabilizing and rehabilitating the former will almost certainly falter if the latter fails to develop a professional and transparent security infrastructure and continues to utilize cross-border interference as a useful and justified tool of statecraft.

Second, criminality and corruption within Pakistan combined with the country's continued culture of Islamist militancy has been a major factor in exacerbating bilateral tensions with India. This is particularly true with regard to Kashmir and the sanctuary Pakistan has given to individuals wanted for terrorism within India, such as Indian mafia don Dawood Ibrahim. More effective institutions for tracking, detaining, and ultimately bringing to justice terrorists, drug syndicates, and other subversives implicated in cross-border activities would undoubtedly help to stabilize government-to-government contacts between Islamabad and Delhi. Over the longer term, this could provide the baseline of trust needed for the development of a more active program of economic and cultural cooperation.

Third, an opaque and nonaccountable security apparatus raises the continual specter of Pakistani nuclear materials finding their way to dangerous nonstate actors. While Pakistan may contend that it has ample control over its fissile material, weapons' designs, and actual weapons, the A.Q. Khan story demonstrates the salience of these concerns, even if the actual details of his activities and the level of state support he enjoyed remain elusive in open-source documents. Significantly, there is little doubt that nonstate actors who seek WMDs see Pakistan as a potential source country. Even if some of these materials and technologies are under adequate control in Pakistan, the consequences of terrorist groups obtaining materials or designs from Pakistan would be enormous and gruesome. It is therefore of paramount interest to the international community to ensure that Pakistan does not become a source of WMD technology for terrorists—either wittingly or unwittingly.

Postscript

This study was written prior to the cataclysmic earthquake that struck northern Pakistan on October 8, 2005. Registering a 7.6 on the Richter scale and centered in Pakistan-administered Kashmir, its effects were also felt in Indian-administered Kashmir and Pakistan's Northern Areas.[1] The Pakistani government estimates that the quake killed some 80,000 of its nationals (in addition to 1,400 people on the Indian-side of Kashmir), injured tens of thousands, and rendered another 3 million homeless. While the disaster does not impact directly on Islamabad's internal security environment—at least as defined in this study—it does have implications for how the country might (or might not) develop over the short-to-medium term.

One immediate ramification has been the quake's effect on the army's reputation, which was clearly shaken when it was unable to provide rapid relief to the affected areas. The delays were due to the military's own personnel losses, the inaccessibility of the terrain in the aftermath of the earthquake, a critical shortage of helicopters, and pressing concerns about protecting the line of control during this crisis. Irrespective of the validity of these reasons, citizens have clearly been dismayed.[2] It is still too early to judge what effect this loss of confidence will have and whether it will be instrumental in opening up greater space and latitude for civilian institutions. The military-dominated regime will no doubt do all it can to maintain its tenacious grip on central power. Moreover, although slow to start, the army did subsequently move to expedite search, rescue, and consequence-management efforts, which has helped to rehabilitate somewhat its national standing.

The earthquake has also had implications for extremist Islamist parties and *tanzeems*, which *did* quickly move to provide assistance to affected areas. Political entities, such as JI, and "militant groups," such as LeT, were among the first to enter disaster zones, playing a vital role in burying the dead and in furnishing the early provision of basic medical help (including surgical procedures), food, shelter, and clothing. They also moved quickly to set up educational facilities for the children whose schools were destroyed. The contribution of these organizations in early emergency response efforts not only laid bare the disingenuousness nature of Islamabad's claims that "there are no militants in Kashmir," but also helped these organizations to gain a stature and legitimacy that they did not previously enjoy. However, it is too early to tell what long-term benefits these militant groups will reap from their post-earthquake efforts and how this will impact on Pakistan's overall internal security environment. While these questions are beyond the scope of this inquiry, they do form the foundation of future research that will be conducted by C. Christine Fair at the Institute.[3]

Notes

A Note on Terms of Reference, Methods, and Sources

1. For more information about this terminological concern, see Guillain Denoeux, "The Forgotten Swamp: Navigating Political Islam," *Middle East Policy*, June 2002; Olivier Roy, *The Failure of Political Islam*, trans. Carol Volk (Cambridge, Mass.: Harvard University Press, 1994). See also note 3 to chapter 12 of *The National Commission on Terrorist Attacks Upon the United States, the 9/11 Commission Report* (New York: W.W. Norton, 2004), 562.

Introduction

1. Both the United States and Pakistan have had different notions of what "partnership" means and both have had different expectations of this partnership. While a robust discussion of this issue is beyond the scope of this study, it has been addressed at great length in C. Christine Fair, *The Counterterrorism Coalitions: Cooperation with Pakistan and India* (Santa Monica, Calif.: RAND, 2004).

2. The authors' use of the appellation GWOT does not imply that the authors agree with the premise of the global war on terrorism or even the widely used moniker. Rather, the authors adopt this term because it is the one that is used in policy circles and remains a priority of the U.S. government.

3. Prior to 9/11, Pakistan's stance on international terrorism was the subject of considerable controversy. Along with Saudi Arabia and the United Arab Emirates, Pakistan was one of only four sovereign states that formally recognized the Taliban regime. Indeed, the Taliban movement itself was very much a creature of Islamabad, with the bulk of its members originally coming from the network of Jamiat-e-Ulema Deobandi *madaris* that had been set up along the Pakistan-Afghanistan border during the anti-Soviet mujahideen war of the 1980s. Numerous militants who have since been connected to the global al-Qaeda network and/or ethnoreligious violence in Central and Southeast Asia are now also known to have been recruited, indoctrinated, and trained in Pakistan, reputedly with the express knowledge, if not active support of, the intelligence and security forces. The reasons for this backing were complex and multifaceted but generally related to geopolitical considerations aimed at establishing strategic depth in South Asia (to offset India's greater military and economic power), consolidating trade and commerce links through Afghanistan, and promoting the regional spread of Islam. Following 9/11, the United States moved decisively to pressure Pakistan to commit to the GWOT. In particular, Washington wanted assistance for its air and land operations in Afghanistan and access to tactical information on al-Qaeda and the Taliban held by the ISI (which, at the time, was generally recognized as having the most complete and comprehensive picture of both groups). To facilitate this objective, the Bush administration pursued a dual-track policy, offering incentives such as debt relief, the suspension of sanctions first imposed in

1990 (after Islamabad declared its nuclear status), and humanitarian assistance, while warning of international ostracization in the event that Pakistan maintained its association with the Taliban. This approach worked. In a landmark address to the country on January 12, 2002, President Musharraf announced that his government was henceforth a full and willing partner in the international coalition against terrorism. For further details, see Ahmed Rashid, *Taliban: Islam, Oil and the New Great Game in Central Asia* (London and New York: I.B. Tauris, 2001), ch. 14; Jessica Stern, "Pakistan's Jihad Culture," *Foreign Affairs* 79, no. 6 (2000); Shawn Howard, "The Afghan Connection: Islamic Extremism in Central Asia," *National Security Studies Quarterly* 6 (Summer 2000); Rajeev Sharma, "Pakistan's Talibinisation," in *The Pakistan Trap*, ed. Rajeev Sharma (New Delhi: UBS Publishers, 2001); "Musharraf's New Pakistan: What the People Think," *Herald* (Pakistan), February 2002, 44–77, and "Musharraf's Move," *Economist*, January 12, 2002, http://www.economist.com/.

4. While the media tends to describe these individuals as being very important to the al-Qaeda organization, former U.S. intelligence analysts have cast doubt on their significance. For instance, a former Africa analyst at the CIA Counterterrorist Center expressed to the authors a firm view that Ghailani, a chief suspect in the 1998 East Africa embassy bombings, is not a senior al-Qaeda commander, regardless of press reporting. The analyst cast similar doubts on the organizational significant of al-Libbi, who is frequently described as al-Qaeda's number-three man in Pakistan, noting there is an ongoing debate regarding his exact role and position in the al-Qaeda hierarchy. However, the analyst did indicate that Sheikh Mohammad and Abu Zubaydah are known to be senior members of the organization. (The analyst's comments were shared with the authors in a formal review of related research in a memo dated January 20, 2006.)

5. As of yet, India and Pakistan have not forged an extradition treaty.

6. See, for instance, Musa Khan Jalalzai, *The Sunni-Shi'a Conflict in Pakistan* (Lahore: Shirkat, 2002).

7. Pakistan maintains it does not provide direct support for militants. However, the majority of South Asia analysts believe otherwise (apart from those in government-backed think tanks within Pakistan). In February 2002, Pakistan claimed that the ISI cell for Afghanistan had been shut down and that the Kashmir cell had been downgraded to an intelligence-gathering detachment. What is notable about this announcement is that Pakistan had long denied even having such cells. See "Pak Shuts Down ISI Cell in Afghanistan," *Tribune* (Chandigarh), February 20, 2002, http://www.tribuneindia.com/2002/20020221/world.htm#8 (accessed October 10, 2005). Later, in 2003, Pakistan announced that the ISI had closed its "Forward Section 23" in Pakistan's Azad (Free) Kashmir. This implied that all training camps and ISI operations offices in that region had been closed. See Syed Saleem Shahzad, "Pakistan-India: Same Game, New Rule," *Asia Times*, November 27, 2003, http://www.atimes.com/atimes/South_Asia/EK27Df03.html (accessed October 10, 2005). So while Pakistan officially denies supporting such operations, its statements suggest otherwise. For further details, see Alexander Evans, "The Kashmir Insurgency: As Bad As It Gets," *Small Wars and Insurgencies* 11 (Spring 2000); Summit Ganguly, *The Crisis in Kashmir*

(Washington, D.C.: Woodrow Wilson Center Press, 1997); Sumantra Bose, *The Challenge in Kashmir: Democracy, Self-Determination and a Just Peace* (New Delhi: Sage Books, 1997); Robert Wirsing, *India, Pakistan and the Kashmir Dispute* (London: Macmillan, 1994); Ashutosh Varshney, "India, Pakistan and Kashmir: Antinomies of Nationalism," *Asian Survey* (November 1991); and Jonah Blank, "Kashmir-Fundamentalism Takes Root," *Foreign Affairs* 78, no. 6 (1999).

8. This view is widely held by U.S. officials both in Washington and at the U.S. embassy in Islamabad. A number of Pakistani journalists, retired and serving army officers, and other commentators interviewed by C. Christine Fair in Pakistan between 2003 and 2005 expressed similar sentiments.

9. See, for instance, Elaine Sciolino and Don Van Natta, "2004 British Raid Sounded Alert on Pakistani Militants," *New York Times*, July, 14, 2005; and Elaine Sciolino and Don Van Natta, "Searching for Footprints," *New York Times*, July 25, 2005.

10. The CPI provides a comparative assessment of national integrity systems based on interviews and surveys aimed at gauging perceived levels of corruption among politicians and public officials. Scores of two or less generally reflect a pervasive problem that is not being met with any concerted countermeasures. In 2003, this ranking was accorded to Bangladesh, Nigeria, Haiti, Paraguay, Myanmar, Tajikistan, Georgia, Cameroon, Azerbaijan, Angola, Kenya, and Tanzania. See Transparency International, "Nine Out of Ten Developing Countries Urgently Need Practical Support to Fight Corruption, Highlights New Index," http://www.transparency kazakhstan.org/english/cpi2003.htm.

11. While the United States has been working with Pakistan to establish a forensics laboratory since 2002, there has been no movement on this front. Pakistan does have some forensic capabilities as described herein. But their capabilities are rudimentary and not consistent with modern evidentiary standards. Notably, the trial of Daniel Pearl's assailants did not include forensic evidence.

12. U.S. State Department officials, interview by Fair, November 2004, and Pakistani officials, interviews by authors, January 2005.

13. See discussion of Indian, Pakistani, and Sri Lankan police capabilities in C. Christine Fair, *Urban Battlefields of South Asia: Lessons Learned from Sri Lanka, India and Pakistan* (Santa Monica, Calif.: RAND, 2004).

14. This assessment is based upon research from numerous sources, including Transparency International–Pakistan, "About TI-Pakistan," http://www.transparency .org.pk/org/abouttipak.htm (accessed July 14, 2005); Nadeem, *The Political Economy of Lawlessness in Pakistan*; and Yasin and Banuri, *The Dispensation of Justice in Pakistan*.

15. See, for instance, World Bank, "Pakistan's Reform Program: Progress and Prospects Report," http://wbln1018.worldbank.org/sar/sa.nsf/083c4661ad49652f852567 d7005d85b8/c3e79a8d2720625385256a090074d943?OpenDocument (accessed February 3, 2003); and International Crisis Group (ICG), *Building Judicial Independence in Pakistan*, ICG Asia Report, no. 86 (Islamabad and Brussels: ICG, 2004).

16. Ashley J. Tellis, "U.S. Strategy: Assisting Pakistan's Transformation," *Washington Quarterly* 28, no. 1 (Winter 2004–2005): 97–116.

17. See Zulfiqar Ali, "Back to the Camps," *Herald* (Pakistan), July 2005.

18. There are critics of this Indian position. There is no extradition treaty between India and Pakistan and thus the expectation that Pakistan would hand over its citizens or even accused Indian citizens is heroic under the prevailing political circumstances.

19. For Musharraf's account, see his personal Web site, "From the Presidents Desk," http://www.presidentofpakistan.gov.pk/FromThePresidentsDesk.aspx (accessed January 5, 2006). See also Iftikar Gilani, "India Releases Data on Kashmir Infiltration," *Daily Times*, August 24, 2005, and "Infiltration Increasing, Says Pranab," *Tribune Chandigarh*, August 24, 2005.

20. U.S. officials, interviews by author, Islamabad, June 2005. Interestingly, one high-ranking Pakistani national security analyst also explained in January 2005 that there would be few alternative options to increasing infiltration given the lack of tangibles in the peace process.

21. Few dedicated analysts of Pakistan see such a collapse as likely in the policy-relevant future. However, because this low-probability event would have enormous and devastating consequences, it is worth mentioning. For a serious discussion about future scenarios for Pakistan, see Stephen P. Cohen, *The Idea of Pakistan* (Washington, D.C.: Brookings Institution Press, 2004).

22. It should be noted that the United States has already been instrumental in instituting certain law enforcement reforms in Pakistan. In FY02, for instance, Washington provided $3 million to help with the creation of a pilot criminal investigation division in Karachi, which may serve as a model for similar units at the provincial level. The Bush administration has also announced a limited scheme of U.S.-based law enforcement training for selected Pakistani police officers and recently pledged to take the lead in setting up a terrorist interdiction program at Karachi International Airport to facilitate the identification of known or suspected terrorists attempting to enter the country.

23. It is difficult for the United States (and arguably most other states) to have a long-term policy given the political exigencies of short-term demands. This is at least in part because the bodies that promulgate policy—the legislative and executive branches—face elections, meaning there is no means of ensuring policy continuity. For this reason, short-term policies often are pursued even if they hurt well-acknowledged long-term goals.

24. The $1.32 billion that Pakistan received in CSF payments between January 2003 and September 2004 was roughly equivalent to one-third of the country's total defense expenditures for that same period. Some U.S. interlocutors suggest that the United States pays Pakistan far in excess of the value of the resources deployed and see these payments as a form of aid. However, Pakistani and other U.S. interlocutors note that it is hard to put an exact price on the amount Pakistan has paid for participating in

the GWOT, especially when factoring in the amount of political capital the government has expended and the substantial loss of life among its military. For more information on CSF, see K. Alan Kronstadt, *Pakistan-U.S. Relations*, Congressional Research Service Report IB94041 (Washington, D.C.: Congressional Research Service, July 26, 2005), http://www.fas.org/sgp/crs/row/IB94041.pdf (accessed October 6, 2005).

25. Pertinent literature in the field is sparse, consisting mostly of anecdotal and press reports, U.S. government summations of extant security programs, and periodic nongovernmental organization (NGO) reports dealing with specific issues, such as educational and judicial reform.

1. Pakistan's Domestic Threat

1. As of early 2006, the situation in Baluchistan has become much more serious. However, it is difficult to obtain accurate information about what is transpiring there in the wake of numerous government efforts to conceal the activities in the region. The central government prefers to characterize the ongoing security operations in the region as "police operations," despite widespread belief that the region is witnessing sustained military force to counter Baloch insurgents. For an excellent account of this crisis and the government's varied responses, see Frédéric Grare, *Pakistan: The Resurgence of Baluch Nationalism*, Carnegie Papers, no. 65 (Washington, D.C.: Carnegie Endowment for International Peace, January 2006), http://www.carnegieendowment.org/files/CP65.Grare.FINAL.pdf (accessed January 30, 2006).

2. Here the authors treat jihadist terrorism separately from sectarian violence even though there are significant commonalities between the two phenomena. Because sectarian and jihadist groups have distinct geneses, sectarian violence is treated separately later in the study.

3. FATA is divided into seven administrative political agencies (Bajaur, Mohmand, Khyber, Orakzai, Kurram, and North and South Waziristan) and six Frontier Regions (Peshawar, Kohat, Bannu, D.I. Khan, Tank, and Lakki Marwat).

4. This is because these treaties were abrogated by the Indian Independence Act of 1947.

5. Government of Pakistan, *Revised Agreement with the Tribal People, Peshawar, 1947*, cited in Rashid Ahmad Khan, "Political Developments in FATA: A Critical Perspective," in *Tribal Areas of Pakistan*, ed. Pervaiz Iqbal Cheema and Maqsudul Hasan Nuri (Islamabad, Islamabad Policy Research Institute, 2005), 27.

6. Pakistan has deployed some 70,000 troops to conduct military operations against suspected terrorists seeking refuge in the tribal areas. It should be noted, however, that many of these personnel are routinely garrisoned along the Afghanistan-Pakistan border; hence, the size of the deployment is not as large as it might seem on paper. See David Rohde et al., "Pakistan Battle Pierces Solitude Of Tribal Area," *New York Times*, March 21, 2004; "Pakistan's Wild Frontier," *Al Jazeera Net*, March 20, 2004, http://english.aljazeera.net/NR/exeres/8BE012FB-EE25-4424-8153-23CE43BE3152.htm

(accessed October 2, 2005); Sharmeen Obaid, "Pakistan: The Hunt for Osama Bin Laden," *Frontline World*, September 14, 2004, http://www.pbs.org/frontlineworld/ elections/pakistan/ (accessed October 2, 2005); Rahimullah Yusufzai, "Waziristan: Bin Laden's Hiding Place?" *BBC News Online*, March 4, 2004, http://news.bbc.co.uk/ 1/hi/world/south_asia/3532841.stm (accessed October 3, 2005); Ahmed Rashid, "Musharraf's Bin Laden Headache," *BBC News Online News*, http://news.bbc.co .uk/2/hi/south_asia/3545985.stm (accessed October 3, 2005); "Pakistan Launches Terror Raid, *CBS News Online*, March 16, 2004, http://www.cbsnews.com/stories/ 2004/03/18/terror/main607118.shtml (accessed October 3, 2005).

7. See Azmat Hayat Khan, "FATA,"in *Tribal Areas of Pakistan: Challenges and Responses*, ed. Pervaiz Iqbal Cheema and Maqsudul Hasan Nuri (Islamabad: Islamabad Policy Institute, 2005), 91–92.

8. Khan, "FATA," 91–92.

9. A *tehsil* is a territorial and administrative subdivision of an agency; each *tehsil* has a political *naib-tehsildar* responsible for controlling the tribes and maintaining law and order within their respective *tehsils*.

10. This common designation has contributed to some confusion about the identity and roles of the two organizations.

11. Khan, "FATA," 93.

12. For a discussion of human rights concerns, see Peter Chalk and C. Christine Fair, "United States Law Enforcement Assistance to Pakistan," in *Securing Reform or Fostering Tyrants*, ed. Olga Oliker, Seth Jones, Peter Chalk, C. Christine Fair, and Rollie Lal (Santa Monica, Calif.: RAND, forthcoming 2006). See also Khan, "FATA," 94–101, and Amnesty International, "Human Rights Abuses in the Search for al-Qa'ida and Taliban in the Tribal Areas," April 1, 2004, http://web.amnesty.org/library/index/ engasa330112004. Notably, this is also mentioned in the U.S. Department of State, Bureau of Democracy, Human Rights and Labor, *Pakistan Country Report on Human Rights Practices—2004*, February 28, 2005, http://www.state.gov/g/drl/rls/hrrpt/ 2004/41743.htm. For an example of robust debate generated by the military oper- ations and the application of the FCR, see the series of entries under "Military Operations in FATA," *PakDef.Info.com* (a Pakistani defense blog and Web site), http:// www.pakdef.info/forum/showthread.php?t=5599.

13. The reader may encounter another term for this group of people, "Pashtun." "Pakhtun" and "Pashtun" are dialectical variants of each other and reference the same group of people. The British introduced the term "Pathan" to describe these people; this term is also still in use. This work will use the term "Pakthun" exclusively, except when citing a source that uses one of the other terms.

14. Scholars at the University of Peshawar, Center for Area Studies, interviews by Fair, February 2004.

15. Ibid.

16. During fieldwork in Pakistan in February 2004, Fair had numerous interviews with individuals with expertise on *pakhtunwali*. Fair also spoke with a former director general of the ISI in September 2005 who shared this more nuanced view of *pakhtunwali*. All concurred that while this hospitality is often described as "unconditional," there are in fact limits to it.

17. For an excellent description of this, see Steve Coll, *Ghost Wars: The Secret History of the CIA, Afghanistan, and Bin Laden, from the Soviet Invasion to September 10, 2001* (New York: Penguin, 2004).

18. Wahabbist ideologies share much in common with Deobandism, which is an important strand of belief in Pakistan.

19. Information about the changed nature of the tribal power relations was gathered by Fair during fieldwork in Pakistan in February 2004 and in August 2005. For a historical account of how the political agents, *maliks*, mullahs, and *jirgas* interacted, see inter alia Brian Robson, *Crisis on the Frontier: The Third Afghan War and the Campaign in Waziristan 1919–1920* (London: Spellmount Publishers, 2004); Alan Warren, *Waziristan, the Faqir of Ipi, and the Indian Army: The North West Frontier Revolt of 1936–37* (Oxford: Oxford University Press, 1999); Akbar S Ahmed, *Order and Conflict in Waziristan: Religion and Politics in an Islamic Society* (1983; repr., Cambridge: Cambridge University Press, 2004); H.C Wylly, *Tribes of Central Asia, from the Black Mountain to Waziristan* (Lahore: Vanguard Books, 1996).

20. Comments made during the Royal United Services Institute conference titled "Tribal Areas of Pakistan: A Haven for Terrorists?" held in London on January 19, 2005. See also Ilyas Khan, "Who Are These People?" *Herald* (Pakistan), April 2004, 60–67.

21. Fair fieldwork in February and March 2004 in Pakistan.

22. Journalists based in Lahore, Islamabad, and Peshawar, interview by Fair, June 2005. See also Paul Haven, "Al-Qaida's No. 3 Man Arrested in Pakistan," *Guardian* (UK), May 4, 2005, http://www.guardian.co.uk/worldlatest/story/0,1280,-4982230,00.html.

23. See James Risen and David Rohde, "Mountains and Border Foil Quest for Bin Laden," *New York Times*, December 13, 2004.

24. ISI and MoI officials, interviews by authors, Rawalpindi and Islamabad, January 2005.

25. Ibid. See also K. Alan Kronstadt and Bruce Vaughn, *Terrorism in South Asia*, Congressional Research Service Report RL32259 (Washington, D.C.: Congressional Research Service, August 9, 2004), 5–6; U.S. Office of the Coordinator for Counterterrorism, *Patterns of Global Terrorism 2002* (Washington, D.C.: U.S. Department of State, April 30, 2003); "Pakistan Asked to Explain Islamic Party Link to Al Qaeda Suspects," Agence France-Presse, March 3, 2003; Kamran Khan and Susan Schmidt, "Key 9/11 Suspect Leaves Pakistan in U.S. Custody," *Washington Post*, September 17, 2002; and Khalid Hasan, "Major Terror Figure Arrested in Karachi,

Flown Out to U.S.," *Daily Times* (Pakistan), May 9, 2002. It should be stressed, however, that the tenure of al-Libbi in FATA suggests that a simultaneous focus on both tribal and urban terrains will be necessary to optimize coalition efforts in the war on terrorism.

26. The Deobandi tradition of Islam is rooted in South Asia (including Afghanistan). Its adherents follow the Hanaffi *fiqah* (juridical school). The tradition is so named because of its origins in the town of Deoband India. The first school of *madaris* associated with this tradition is Darul Uloom Doband.

27. All of these groups were proscribed in 2002 and have since operated under various front names, including Jamaat-ul-Furqan (JeM), Jamaat-ul-Dawa (LeT), and Harakat-ul Mujahideen al-Aalami (HuM). These groups, under their new names, were again proscribed in 2003, with one exception: Jamaat-ul-Dawa (JuD) was only put on a watch list. JuD maintains it is not a militant organization and is free to operate openly. See Shaukat Piracha, "3 More Religious Outfits Banned," November 21, 2003, *Daily Times* (Pakistan), http://www.dailytimes.com.pk/default.asp?page=story_21-11-2003_pg1_3 (accessed October 10, 2005). For further details on the Kashmir conflict, see Alexander Evans, "The Kashmir Insurgency: As Bad As It Gets," *Small Wars and Insurgencies* 11 (Spring 2000); Summit Ganguly, *The Crisis in Kashmir* (Washington, D.C.: Woodrow Wilson Center Press, 1997); Sumantra Bose, *The Challenge in Kashmir: Democracy, Self-Determination and a Just Peace* (New Delhi: Sage Books, 1997); Robert Wirsing, *India, Pakistan and the Kashmir Dispute* (London: Macmillan, 1994); Asutosh Varshney, "India, Pakistan and Kashmir: Antinomies of Nationalism," *Asian Survey* (November 1991); and Jonah Blank, "Kashmir-Fundamentalism Takes Root," *Foreign Affairs* 78, no. 6 (1999).

28. A number of commentaries germane to these groups exist. For useful data points, see the *South Asia Terrorism Portal*, http://www.satp.org, and the South Asia Analysis Group, http://www.saag.org.

29. Pakistani journalists and analysts, interviews by Fair, June 2005. See also Amir Mir, *True Face of the Jihadis* (Lahore: Mashall Books, 2004); Zaffar Abbas, "What Happened," *Herald* (Pakistan), June 2005; John Lancaster and Kamran Khan, "Investigation of Attacks on Musharraf Points to Pakistani Group," *Washington Post*, January 14, 2004; and Salmon Masood, "Musharraf Vows Crackdown," *National Post* (Canada), December 26, 2003.

30. See also Mir, *True Face of the Jihadis*. Fair's interviews with journalists and other terrorism analysts in January and June 2005 elicited data that comports with this narrative.

31. Fair and Chalk fieldwork in January 2005 and June 2005. The expression "calibrate the jihad" is fairly common among analysts in Pakistan. This expression refers to the belief among Pakistani security managers that it can control the tempo of the militancy in Indian-administered Kashmir by imposing operational constraints on the militant groups. For another discussion of this phenomenon, see Ashley J. Tellis, C. Christine

Fair, and Jamison Jo Medby, *Limited Conflicts Under the Nuclear Umbrella—Indian and Pakistani Lessons from the Kargil Crisis* (Santa Monica, Calif.: RAND, 2001).

32. During that visit, President Musharraf pledged to Armitage that Pakistan would immediately and permanently end cross-border infiltration of terrorists into Jammu and Kashmir. This was conveyed to New Delhi by Armitage during a June 8, 2002, phone conversation. See Government of India, Ministry of External Affairs, "Statement on Telephone Call by US Secretary of State and on Visit of US Deputy Secretary of State Richard Armitage," June 8, 2002, http://meaindia.nic.in/event/2002/06/08 event01.htm (accessed October 8, 2005). Unfortunately, this pledge appears to have been quickly broken according to M. Ilyas Khan, "The Waiting Game," *Herald* (Pakistan), July 2003; and M. Ilyas Khan, "Business as Usual," *Herald* (Pakistan), July 2003.

33. Data drawn from Fair's participation in a research project sponsored by the Naval Postgraduate School investigating the cause and consequences of the 2001–02 Indian-Pakistan military crisis. Fair attended sessions in Islamabad in June 2005 and at Monterey in August 2005. These findings will appear in a forthcoming volume edited by Peter Lavoy.

34. This assessment draws from Fair's interviews with political scientists and journalists in Lahore, Islamabad, and Peshawar in June 2005. See also Muhammad Amir Rana, *The A to Z of Jehadi Organizations in Pakistan* (Lahore: Mashal, 2004) and Mir, *True Face of the Jehadis*. For obvious reasons, Pakistan will not agree with this assessment.

35. "Enlightened moderation" (EM) is based on a two-prong strategy that aims at (1) domestic internal reform and renewal (focusing especially on the health, education, and judicial sectors) and (2) encouragement of the international community to both help resolve drivers of Islamist radicalism (such as the Palestinian-Israeli conflict) and engage countries seeking economic development. President Musharraf has explicitly touted EM as the guiding framework for the future direction of Pakistani domestic and foreign policy. See Pervez Musharraf, "A Plea for Enlightened Moderation: Muslims Must Raise Themselves Up through Individual Achievement and Socioeconomic Emancipation," *Washington Post*, June 1, 2004. See also Hasan-Askari Rizvi, "A Moderate and Enlightened Pakistan," *Daily Times* (Pakistan), January 17, 2005. MoI officials, interviews by authors, Islamabad, January 2005. See also Fair, "Militant Recruitment in Pakistan," *Studies in Conflict and Terrorism* 27, no. 6 (November-December 2004): 493; Kronstadt and Vaughn, *Terrorism in South Asia*, 8–9; Ahmed Rashid, "Islamists Impose Taliban-Type Morals Monitors," *Daily Telegraph* (UK), June 3, 2003; "The Wild Frontier," *Economist*, April 12, 2003; and "Oh, What a Lovely Ally," *Economist*, October 19, 2002.

36. See Mir, *True Face of the Jihadis*; also derived from Fair interviews in June 2005. See also Abbas, "What Happened"; John Lancaster and Kamran Khan, "Investigation of Attacks on Musharraf Points to Pakistani Group," *Washington Post*, January 14, 2004; and Salmon Masood, "Musharraf Vows Crackdown," *National Post* (Canada), December 26, 2003.

37. See Amir Mir, *True Face of the Jihadis*; also derived from Fair interviews in June 2005. See also Abbas, "What Happened"; John Lancaster and Kamran Khan, "Investigation of Attacks on Musharraf Points to Pakistani Group," *The Washington Post*, January 14, 2004; and Salmon Masood, "Musharraf Vows Crackdown," *National Post* (Canada), December 26, 2003; Mubashir Zaidi, "Militant Flourishes in Plain Sight," *Los Angeles Times*, January 25, 2004; Amy Waldman, "Pakistan Arrests Militant With Ties to Taliban," *New York Times*, August 9, 2004; Juliette Terzieff, "Assassination Tries Linked to al-Qaeda," *San Francisco Chronicle*, January 16, 2004.

38. The authors have spoken with representatives of numerous U.S. government officials about this issue. For an example of the kind of evidence that is often marshaled, see Arif Jamal, *News on Sunday*, November 10, 2002. Jamal gives an excellent account of the kinds of statements made at the LeT gathering.

39. LeT's anti-Western positions have been clearly articulated in its published and publicly available materials (including books, pamphlets, poster art, DVDs, and CDs) for years. Unfortunately, these materials remain largely untapped by analysts. For more information about the organization's literature, see forthcoming work on this subject by Husain Haqqani and C. Christine Fair. (Fair has been collecting the organization's literature since the mid-1990s.) It is notable that U.S. government analysts who have spent most of their career focusing on Pakistan and its environs tend to discount the assertion that LeT is globalizing and share the authors' assessment that LeT has always claimed to be global in outlook but has retained a distinctly local focus. Little or no credence is given here to the rare and odd account of U.S.-based LeT cells, such as the Virginia "paint-ball" cell.

40. Intelligence Bureau (IB) and National Security Council Advisory Board members, interviews by authors, Delhi, September 2002.

41. Kronstadt and Vaughn, *Terrorism in South Asia*, 5; U.S. Office of the Coordinator for Counterterrorism, *Patterns of Global Terrorism 2002*.

42. Indian sources have spearheaded these claims. For instance, see "Suicide Squad to Battle Western Forces: LeT," *Times of India*, June 13, 2004, and Praveen Swami, "Riding the Jehadi Tiger," *Kashmir Herald On the Web* 3, no. 11 (May 2004), http://www.kashmirherald.com/featuredarticle/jehaditiger.html (accessed September 23, 2005). Despite these allegations, there have been no public announcements of LeT detainments in Iraq. See Kaushik Kapisthalam, "Outside View: Pakistani Jihadis in Iraq," *Washington Times Online*, July 5, 2004, http://washingtontimes.com/upi-breaking/20040705-123700-2711r.htm (accessed September 23, 2005).

43. See, for instance, Luke Harding and Rosie Cowan, "Pakistan Militants Linked to London Attacks," *Guardian* (UK), July 19, 2005; Peter Foster and Nasir Malick, "Suicide Bombers Flew to Pakistan Together," *Daily Telegraph* (UK), July 19, 2005; Alan Cowell and Don Van Natta, "4 From Britain Carried Out Terror Blasts, Police Say," *New York Times*, July 13, 2005; and Elaine Sciolino and Don Van Natta, "2004 British Raid Sounded Alert on Pakistani Militants," *New York Times*, July 14, 2005. The individual in question was Shehzad Tanweer, who was thought to have traveled to

Pakistan no less than four times between 2001 and the perpetration of the martyr operation in July 2005. Besides allegedly visiting LeT headquarters, he is known to have made contact with JeM through Osama Nazir, a JeM member who was arrested in December 2004 in connection with the bombing of a church in Islamabad.

44. Veteran Pakistan analyst, in discussion with Fair, September 2005.

45. Stern, "Pakistan's Jihad Culture."

46. Peter W. Singer, *Pakistan's Madrassahs: Ensuring a System of Education not Jihad,* Analysis Papers 41 (Washington, D.C.: Brookings Institution, 2001).

47. Press reports in October 2005 claimed that there are at least 13,000 or 14,000 *madaris.* See Zaffar Abbas, "Pakistan Madrassa Row 'Resolved,'" *BBC News Online,* September 23, 2005, http://news.bbc.co.uk/2/hi/south_asia/4275848.stm (accessed October 3, 2005); "Pakistan's Madrassas Agree to Register with Govt by Year-End— Official," *Forbes.com,* September 23, 2005, http://www.forbes.com/finance/feeds/afx/2005/09/23/afx2240820.html (accessed October 3, 2005).

48. MoI officials, interviews by authors, Islamabad, January 2005. However, this notion of registering *madaris* has been part of an ongoing challenge in Pakistan. Even before 2001, Pakistan tried to institute *madarassah* reform with no success. More recently, Pakistan has introduced various efforts to track *madarassah* funding and control foreign students' enrollment. Although the government usually claims early success, these efforts have led to few tangible results. As evidence of this, each such effort is inevitably followed by another.

49. See review of this literature in Tahir Andrabi et al., "Religious School Enrollment in Pakistan: A Look at the Data" (working paper, World Bank, February 2005), http://econ.worldbank.org/external/default/main?pagePK=64165259&piPK=64165421&menuPK=64166093&theSitePK=469372&entityID=000112742_20050228152509/ (accessed October 3, 2005).

50. Ibid.

51. See Rana, *The A to Z of Jehadi Organizations in Pakistan.* Rana provides an exhaustive overview of the various *madaris* that are linked to militant organizations.

52. U.S. State Department, Office of the Coordinator for Counterterrorism, and MoI officials, interviews by authors, Washington, D.C., and Islamabad, December 2004– January 2005.

53. Fair, "Militant Recruitment in Pakistan," 494; Nadeem Malik, "15 to 20 pc Madaris Impart Military Training: WB," *News International* (Pakistan), August 2, 2002; "Editorial: Retreating on the Madrassas," *Daily Times* (Pakistan), August 5, 2002; Robert Looney, "Strategic Insight—A U.S. Strategy for Achieving Stability in Pakistan: Expanding Educational Opportunities," September 2, 2002, http://www.ccc.nps.navy.mil/rsepResources/si/sept02/southAsia.asp. At an August 2004 meeting on international Islamist terrorism at the Center for Strategic and International Studies,

Pakistan analysts discussed the possibility that *madaris* are now providing basic militant training as the operation of camps has become increasingly difficult.

54. Singer, "Pakistan's Madrassahs," and ICG, *Pakistan: Madrassahs, Extremism and the Military*, Asia Report, no. 36 (Islamabad/Brussels: ICG, 2002).

55. Fair, "Militant Recruitment in Pakistan," 494. See also Stern, "Pakistan's Jihad Culture." See also A.H. Nayyar and Ahmed Salim, *The Subtle Subversion: The State of Curricula and Textbooks in Pakistan* (Islamabad: Sustainable Development Policy Institute, 2003); K.K. Aziz, *Murder of History: A Critique of History Textbooks Used in Pakistan* (Islamabad: Renaissance Publishing House, 1998). Sentiments of this sort were also expressed during authors' interviews with the FIA and senator representatives, Islamabad, January 2005.

56. ISI and MI officials, interviews by authors, Rawalpindi and Islamabad, January 2005.

57. "PM Assures Review of Foreigners Issue," *Daily Times* (Pakistan), September 24, 2005, http://www.dailytimes.com.pk/default.asp?page=story_24-9-2005_pg1_2 (accessed October 3, 2005).

58. The remaining 30 percent of Pakistan's students attend private schools.

59. Fair, "Militant Recruitment in Pakistan," 494. For more on this, see Nayyar and Salim, *The Subtle Subversion*; Aziz, *Murder of History*. Sentiments of this sort were also expressed during authors' interviews with the FIA and senator representatives, Islamabad, January 2005.

60. See Husain Haqqani. *Pakistan: Between Mosque and Military* (Washington, D.C.: Carnegie Endowment for International Peace, 2005).

61. Khaled Ahmed, "Debate on Textbooks, Pakistani Style," *Friday Times* (Pakistan), April 16, 2004; Zubeida Mustafa, "A Curriculum of Hatred," *Link*, April 9, 2004, http://www.pakistanlink.com/Letters/2004/April04/09/02.html (accessed October 5, 2005).

62. "Khalid Sheikh under FBI Interrogation," *News International*; "Bin Ladin Alive, Says Captured Leader," *Guardian* (UK); Abrar Saeed, "Top al-Qaeda Operative Arrested in Pindi." JI vigorously denies that this arrest occurred at the home of Qudoos. See "Pakistan's Islamic Party Denies Links with al-Qaeda," Deutsche Presse-Agentur, March 5, 2003.

63. Parties in the MMA include Jamiat Ulema-e-Islam (JUI), JI, Jamiat Ulema-e-Pakistan (JUP), Jamiat Ahle Hadith (JAH), and Islami Tehreek Pakistan (ITP). The MMA rules the provincial assembly of the NWFP outright and shares power with the King's Party (PML-Q) in Baluchistan.

64. Tim McGirk and Hanna Bloch, "Has Pakistan Tamed Its Spies?" *Time*, May 6, 2003, 32. Some accounts allege this individual was a colonel.

65. David Rohde, "Two Years Later: Islamic Ally: Questions Grow on Pakistan's Commitment to Fight Taliban," *New York Times*, September 10, 2003; Ahmed Rashid, "Pakistan Army Officers Arrested in Terror Swoop," *Telegraph*, September 1, 2003.

66. McGirk and Bloch, "Has Pakistan Tamed Its Spies?"

67. Abbas, "What Happened," 71.

68. Ibid.

69. Pakistan Army official, interview by Fair, Washington, D.C., June 22, 2005, and U.S. foreign service officer who spent most of his career in Pakistan, in discussion with Fair, June 22, 2005. The army routinely scrutinizes (through extensive background investigations by both the ISI and Military Intelligence) officers with the rank of colonel or above. However, lower-ranking officers and enlisted personnel are not subject to such scrutinzation.

70. Interlocutors interviewed in February and March 2003 in Islamabad and Peshawar were of the belief that this was indeed an unusual cell and did not likely suggest deeper army support. For more current accounts, see Zaffar Abbas, "Pakistan's Military-Militant Link," *BBC News Online*, June 16, 2005, http://news.bbc.co.uk/go/pr/fr/-/world/south_asia/4094716.stm; Zaffar Abbas, "The Pakistani Al-Qaeda," *Herald* (Pakistan), August 2004; M. Ilyas Khan, "Ready to Rumble," *Herald* (Pakistan), August 2004. See also Zaffar Abbas, "The Fifth Column," *Herald* (Pakistan), June 2005.

71. British Security Service JTAC officials, interview by Chalk, London, January 2005. See also Juliette Terzieff, "Assassination Tries Linked to al-Qaeda," *San Francisco Chronicle*, January 16, 2004; Salman Masood, "Musharraf Vows Renewed Crackdown," *National Post* (Canada), December 26, 2003; John Lancaster and Kamran Khan, "Investigation of Attacks on Musharraf Points to Pakistani Group," *Washington Post*, January 14, 2004; and Paul Watson and Mubashir, "Militant Flourishes in Plain Sight," *Los Angeles Times*, January 25, 2004.

72. Alex Spillers and Philip Broughton, "Al-Qa'eda Suicide Bomb Kills 14," *Daily Telegraph* (UK), June 27, 2005; and "Karachi Bomb 'Terrorist Murders,'" *CNN.Com*, May 09, 2002, http://archives.cnn.com/2002/WORLD/asiapcf/south/05/08/pakistan.bombing/?related (accessed June 27, 2005).

73. Political scientists and terrorism analysts, interviews by Fair, Lahore and Islamabad, June 2005.

74. See Haqqani, *Pakistan: Between Mosque and Military*.

75. Since Musharraf came to power in 1999, the PPP and PML are no longer functioning as viable and distinct political bodies. As a result, the present government has attempted to forge new governing arrangements out of component cooperative elements drawn from the two parties.

76. Sentiments expressed during a roundtable meeting with the National Security Council Advisory Board, Delhi, September 2002. See also "Another Provocation," *Economist*, January 26, 2002; Celia Dugger and Barry Bearak, "Indian Officials Tie

Attack to a Pakistani-Based Group, But the FBI Chief Demurs," *New York Times*, January 23, 2002; "Eyeball to Eyeball," *Economist*, January 5, 2002; and Rajiv Chanrasekaran and Rama Lashmi, "New Delhi Lays Blame," *Washington Post*, December 29, 2001.

77. Political-military analysts and journalists, interviews by Fair, Islamabad, June 2005.

78. This new Indian warfare doctrine calls for rapid deployment of Integrated Battle Groups comprised of elements from the army, air force, and, if need be, navy. These battle groups will be capable of operating under several kinds of contingencies. In a serious departure from its past military planning, a "decisive military victory is no longer the exclusive goal of war against Pakistan." For more information, see *Bharat Rakshak Monitor* 6, no. 6 (2004), http://www.bharat-rakshak.com/MONITOR/ISSUE6-6/patel.html (accessed January 30, 2006). For other related references, see Rajesh Basrur, "Coercive Diplomacy in a Nuclear Environment," presented at the Prospects for Peace in South Asia: 2nd Conference on South Asian Security, January 21 and 22, 2003, Bechtel Conference Center, Stanford University; Y.I. Patel, "Dig Vijay to Divya Astra—a Paradigm Shift in the Indian Army's Doctrine," *Bharat Rakshak Monitor* 6, no. 6 (2004), http://www.bharat-rakshak.com/MONITOR/ISSUE6-6/patel.html (accessed October 3, 2005).

79. Sectarian violence in the Pakistani context refers essentially to organized and militant religious activism, the specific aim of which is to safeguard the interests of particular Sunni and Shi'a communities. Seyyed Vali Reza Nasr, "International Politics, Domestic Imperatives and Identity Mobilization," *Comparative Politics* 2, no. 2 (2000): 171–72. For more on the general mobilization of ethnic and sectarian identity, see Donald Horowitz, *Ethnic Groups in Conflict* (Berkeley: University of California Press, 1985).

80. Several other militant sectarian groups exist in Pakistan. Other Sunni groups include the Jhangvi Tigers, the Al-Haq Tigers, Al-Farooq, the Al-Badr Foundation, Allahu Akbar, and Tanzeemul Haq; other Shi'a groups include the Immamia Organization, the Imamia Students Organization, the Aldamar Students organization, the Abuzar Ghaffari Group, the Mukhtar Force, and the Wafq Ulema-Shia. However, these various groups have either largely failed to exert a decisive operational impact in Pakistan or have been subsumed within the organizational structures of the SSP/LeJ or the TJP/SMP.

81. Many of these Islamizing initiatives were undertaken first by Z.A. Bhutto following Pakistan's defeat in the 1971 war. On differences between Sunni and Shi'a interpretations of Islamic law and jurisprudence, see N.J. Coulson, *A History of Islamic Law* (Edinburgh: Edinburgh University Press, 1964), 113–119.

82. Charles Kennedy, "Islamization and Legal Reform in Pakistan, 1979–1989," *Pacific Affairs* 63 (spring 1990): 62–77; Mumtaz Ahmad, "Islam and the States: The Case of Pakistan," in *Religious Challenge to the State*, ed. Matthew Moen and L. Gustafson (Philadelphia: Temple University Press, 1992), 230–40.

83. Shi'a make up roughly 20 percent of Pakistan's population, with Sunnis constituting approximately 70 percent. Christians and Hindus constitute the bulk of the remaining 10 percent. Unfortunately, the exact number of Shi'a is unknown as areas where they are predominant are not enumerated in Pakistan's census (e.g., in Pakistan's Northern Areas). Thus, the percentage of Shi'a is often put between 15 and 25 percent. See discussion in C. Christine Fair, "Islam and Politics in Pakistan," in *The Muslim World and the United States After 9/11 and the Iraq War*, ed. Angel Rabasa (Santa Monica, Calif.: RAND, 2004).

84. Jalalzai, *The Sunni-Shi'a Conflict*, 260–61; Muhammad Qasim Zaman, "Sectarianism in Pakistan: The Radicalization of Shi'a and Sunni Identities," *Modern Asian Studies* 32, no. 3 (1998): 692–93; Nasr, "International Politics, Domestic Imperatives and Identity Mobilization," 175–76. The Shi'a also argued that the central government would not distribute these resources equitably.

85. Nasr, "International Politics, Domestic Imperatives and Identity Mobilization," 176; Zaman, "Sectarianism in Pakistan," 687–716.

86. Nasr, "International Politics, Domestic Imperatives and Identity Mobilization," 176; Jalalzai, *The Sunni-Shi'a Conflict*, 261.

87. Zaman, "Sectarianism in Pakistan," 70–102; Rana, *A to Z of Jehadi Organizations in Pakistan*, 192–93, 195–203 "Sipah-e-Sahaba Pakistan, Terrorist Group of Pakistan," *South Asia Terrorism Portal*, http://www.satp.org/satporgtp/countries/pakistan/terrorist outfits/ssp.htm.

88. Naqvi was arrested in 1996 and is currently in prison serving concurrent sentences on some thirty charges of murder.

89. The SMP also stresses the need to completely overhaul Pakistan's social, economic, and political system—including Islamabad's reputed slavery to the dictates of Western "imperialist powers"—to ensure the emergence of a leadership committed to the creation of a state predicated on the observance of "pure Islam." See Zaman, "Sectarianism in Pakistan," 696–97.

90. "Sipah-e-Mohammed Pakistan, Terrorist Group of Pakistan"; Rana, *A to Z of Jehadi Organizations in Pakistan*, 414–24. See also "Sectarian Violence in Pakistan," *South Asia Terrorism Portal*, http://www.satp.org/satporgtp/countries/pakistan/database/sect-killing.htm. The LeJ has also carried out attacks against other religious groups, including the Ahmadiyya sect (which was declared a non-Muslim minority under Pakistan's 1974 constitution) and Christians.

91. During the 1990s, a considerable component of Shi'a militant training took place in Pakistan. However, this was curtailed following the Taliban's consolidation of power in 1996. BBC correspondent, interview by authors, Islamabad, January 2005.

92. Various governmental and nongovernmental Indian officials, interviews by authors, Delhi, September 2002. See also "Sipah-e-Mohammed, Terrorist Group of Pakistan"; and Sundeep Waslekar, Leena Pillai, and Shabnam Siddiqui, *The Future of Pakistan* (Mumbai: International Centre for Peace Initiatives, 2002), 61.

93. Ajmal has been in prison since 2002. For more information about LeJ, see the entry for LeJ's group profile in the MIPT Terrorism Knowledgebase, "Lashkar-e-Jhangvi," http://tkb.org/Group.jsp?groupID=65 (accessed October 3, 2005); Rana, *A to Z of Jehadi Organizations in Pakistan*, 203–208; and "Lashkar-e-Jhangvi, Terrorist Group of Pakistan," *South Asia Terrorism Portal*, http://www.satp.org/satporgtp/countries/pakistan/terroristoutfits/lej.htm.

94. BBC correspondent, interview by authors, Islamabad, January 2005. See also Roger Howard, "Probing the Ties That Bind Militant Islam," *Jane's Intelligence Review* 12 (February 2000): 38; "Lashkar-e-Jhangvi, Terrorist Group of Pakistan," *South Asia Terrorism Portal*, http://www.satp.org (last accessed March 6, 2006).

95. See, for instance, data on the *South Asia Terrorism Portal*, http://www.satp.org.

96. Ibid.

97. Such instances were especially rife in 2004. See "'Suicide Attack' Hits Karachi Mosque," *BBC News Online*, May 7, 2004, http://newsvote.bbc.co.uk/; "Killing of Sunni Cleric Spurs Riots in Pakistan," *Los Angeles Times*, May 31, 2004; "Pakistani Mosque Bombed; 16 Killed," *Los Angeles Times*, June 01, 2004; "Eleven Killed in Karachi Attack," *BBC News Online*, June 10, 2004, http://newsvote.bbc.co.uk; "Pak on High Alert as Militant Reveals Plot to Attack Shiites," Associated Press, July 02, 2004; "Dozens Killed in Pakistan Blast," *BBC News Online*, October 7, 2004, http://newsvote.bbc.co.uk; Salmon Masood, "Pakistan Bans Public Meetings After 40 Die in a Car Bombing," *New York Times*, October 8, 2004; and Salmon Masood, "Suicide Bomber Kills 3 Others at a Shiite Mosque in Pakistan," *New York Times*, October 11, 2004.

98. Waslekar, Pillai, and Siddiqui, *The Future of Pakistan*, 59.

99. U.S. State Department officials, interview by authors, November 2004.

100. National Security Council Advisory Board members, interview by authors, Delhi, September 2002, and BBC correspondent, interview by authors, Islamabad, January 2005.

101. Despite the horrific law-and-order situation in Karachi, the Karachi Stock Exchange (KSE) has remained in recent years one of the world's highest-performing stock exchanges. In 2002, *Business Week* and *USA Today* declared the KSE to be the "Best Performing Stock Market of The World For the Year 2002." As of December 31, 2004, the KSE listed some 700 companies with a total market capitalization of Rs 1,723.45 billion ($29 billion). For more information, see the KSE's official Web site, http://www.kse.com.pk/kse4/index.html (accessed August 22, 2005). In addition, Pakistan generally has performed well at the macroeconomic level despite local disturbances caused by violence. See Asian Development Bank, "Pakistan: Economic Update (July 2004-March 2005)," http://www.adb.org/Documents/Economic_Updates/PAK/default.asp (accessed August 22, 2005). For a more historical overview of the economic effects of sectarianism, see Zaman, "Sectarianism in Pakistan," 713–14.

102. The Golden Crescent embraces Afghanistan, Pakistan, India, and eastern Iran.

103. The United Nations declared Pakistan a "poppy-free nation" in 2001. That said, a certain amount of drug production continues to take place in the country. The U.S. government estimated that roughly 3,000 hectares of poppies were cultivated in 2003, generating a base crop potentially able to yield 62 metric tons of opium. See Office of Narcotics and International Law Enforcement Affairs, "Southwest Asia," *International Narcotics Control Strategy Report, 2003* (Washington, D.C.: U.S. Department of State, March 2004).

104. Afghan opiates are also smuggled through the Central Asian republics of Uzbekistan, Kazakhstan, Kyrgyzstan, Turkmenistan, and, especially, Tajikistan. The main trafficking route appears to run from Afghanistan, via the Tajik districts of Gorno-Badakhshan, Shurobod, Moskovski, and Panj, to the Ferghana Valley in Uzbekistan. From there the narcotics are redistributed and shipped through Kazakhstan and Kyrgyzstan to the European market by way of Russia and the Baltic States. A secondary route runs from Afghanistan through Turkmenistan to the Caspian Sea and from there on to the Balkans via Armenia, Azerbaijan, and Turkey. See Chalk, "Non-Military Security in the Wider Middle East," *Studies in Conflict and Terrorism* 26, no. 3 (2003): 199; and United Nations Office on Drugs and Crime, *The Opium Economy in Afghanistan: An International Problem* (New York: United Nations, 2003), 154.

105. See Office of Narcotics and Law Enforcement Affairs, "Southwest Asia," *International Narcotics Control Strategy Report, 2004* (Washington D.C.: U.S. Department of State, March 2005). For historical assessments, see Pierre-Arnaud Chouvy, "Afghan Opium Production Predicted to Reach New High," *Jane's Intelligence Review* (October 2004): 29; Susanna Loof, "U.N. Agency Warns Afghanistan Over Opium," *Guardian* (UK), October 29, 2003; and Eric Schmitt, "Afghan's Gains Threatened by Drug Traffic," *New York Times*, December 11, 2004. Most of the poppy fields in Afghanistan are located in the foothills of the Spin Ghar mountains, Nangarhar Province, which borders Pakistan to the east—a region that is thought to account for a full 60 percent of all the heroin trafficked to Europe. The overall income earned from Afghan production and trafficking is estimated at around $2.8 billion, which equates to roughly one-third of the country's total economy.

106. As shown in table 2, the Taliban's opium ban resulted in a net output of only 74 metric tons of opium gum in 2001, substantially lower than the average annual yield of 1,851 metric tons recorded between 1992 and 2000. See also Chalk, "Non-Military Security in the Wider Middle East," 198; Chouvy, "Afghan Opium Production Predicted to Reach New High," 31; and "Southwest Asia," *International Narcotics Control Strategy Report, 2002* (Washington, D.C.: U.S. Department of State, March 2003).

107. With the start of OEF, the United States was initially prepared to condone opium production in Afghanistan largely because cultivation and refining took place in areas controlled by the Northern Alliance or held by local commanders whose support was deemed essential to fight the Taliban and al-Qaeda. It should be noted, however, that since 2004, Washington has actively moved to curtail the Afghan drug trade both because of its perceived threat to the country's nascent democratic institutions and because heroin profits are now thought to be funding militant opposition groups in

Afghanistan, such as Gulbuddin Kekmatyar's Hezb-I-Islami, which was at the forefront of attempts to disrupt the national elections during October 2004. ANF officials, interview by authors, Rawalpindi, January 2005. See also Chouvy, "Afghan Opium Production Predicted to Reach New High," 29–30.

108. Under the Afghan salaam loan system, peasants without capital traditionally borrow important sums of money against future expected crop earnings, including from poppies, which can be sold one or two years before they are actually harvested—typically at half the price of their market value. The Taliban's enforced opium ban thus had a heavy impact on the plant's farmers, many of whom experienced significant financial arrears as a result of being unable to cover advanced credit. Accordingly, following the removal of Mullah Omar's regime, poppy growers immediately moved to increase poppy cultivation in order to run down accumulated debt as quickly as possible. Chouvy, "Afghan Opium Production Predicted to Reach New High," 31.

109. See section on "Southwest Asia," *International Narcotics Control Strategy Report, 2003.*

110. A total of seventy-two metric tons of heroin was seized in the wider Afghan opiate containment zone, which includes Pakistan, Iran, Uzbekistan, Tajikistan, and Russia. ANF officials, interview by authors, Rawalpindi, January 2005. See also "Southwest Asia," *International Narcotics Control Strategy Report, 2003;* "Tonne of Heroin Worth $8.4 Million Seized in Pakistan," Reuters, November 13, 2003.

111. See Kshitif Prabha, "Narco-Terrorism: The Case of the Golden Crescent," in *Rise of Terrorism and Secessionism in Eurasia,* ed. V.D. Chopra (New Delhi: Gyan Publishing House, 2001), 318; "Two Elections: New Hopes and Old Frustrations," *South Asia Monitor,* November 1, 2002; "Oh, What a Lovely Ally," *Economist,* October 17, 2002. It is important to note, however, that officials within Pakistan's ANF reject this depiction of a lack of state penetration, arguing that they have freely entered these areas and have carried out effective operations there. For these officials, the more relevant challenge to operating in the area stems from inadequate strength, aerial mobility, and intelligence acquisition. ANF director general, interview by authors, Rawalpindi, February 2005.

112. Karachi and Qasim are the main ports of concern, although a number of smaller fishing enclaves and inlets along the Makran coast have also proven vulnerable to drug traffic, especially shipments bound for the Persian Gulf states.

113. ANF officials, interview by authors, Rawalpindi, January 2005.

114. ANF officials note that strategic consignments passing through Baluchistan and onward to the seaports typically involve amounts of 1,000 kilograms. Director general of the ANF, in personal communication with Fair in February 2005 to clarify points raised during our meeting in January 2005.

115. Chalk, "Non-Military Security in the Wider Middle East," 199; Ed Blanche, "Iran Struggles With Narcotics Scourge," *Jane's Intelligence Review* (October 2000): 33; *Illicit Drugs Situation in the Regions Neighboring Afghanistan and the Response of the ODCCP*

(Vienna: United Nations Office for Drug Control and Crime Prevention, October 2002), 12.

116. Even in Turkey, for instance, a kilogram of heroin sold in Pakistan for $2,000 would fetch $10,000. See Rowan Scarborough, "Osama bin Laden a 'Narco-Terrorist,'" *Washington Times*, January 22, 2004.

117. Eric Schmitt, "Afghan's Gains Threatened by Drug Traffic," *New York Times*, December 11, 2004.

118. "Southwest Asia," *International Narcotics Control Strategy Report, 2003*. For an account of the various facets of the interaction between the South Asian and African drug trade, see Mark Shaw, "West African Criminal Networks in South and Southern Africa," *African Affairs* 101 (2002): 291–316; and "South Africa Becomes Major Hub in Global Drug Trafficking," *Jane's Intelligence Review* (July 2005): 38–43

119. U.S. State Department officials, interviews by authors, Washington, D.C., November 2004, and ANF officials, interviews by authors, Rawalpindi, January 2005.

120. There is currently no concerted legal framework for addressing money laundering in Pakistan, largely due to official resistance to criminalizing tax evasion and corruption, both of which are highly lucrative. U.S. State Department officials, interview by authors, Washington, D.C., November 2004.

121. *Illicit Drugs Situation in the Regions Neighboring Afghanistan and the Response of the ODCCP*, 27.

122. "Southwest Asia," *International Narcotics Control Strategy Report, 2003*; "Dawn on the Internet," *Dawn*, October 6, 2004, http://dawn.com/2004/10/06/nat20.htm; Colonel G.H. Niaz, "Stop the Spread of Drug Addiction in Pakistan," *Pakistan News Service*, June 27, 2004, http://paknews.com/art1jun-27.html; Sara Alam, "The Rising Toll of Drug Addicts," *Spiros Tzelepis*, July-August 2002, http://users.otenet.gr/~tzelepisk/yc/24.htm.

123. ANF officials, interview by authors, January 2005.

124. One study undertaken for the *Journal of Drug and Alcohol Dependence* showed that needle sharing among drug users in Pakistan has increased threefold since the overthrow of the Taliban in 2001. See Steffanie Strathdee, "The Rise in Needle Sharing among Drug Users in Pakistan during the Afghanistan War," *Journal of Drug and Alcohol Dependence* (July 2003). See also Ania Litchtarowicz, "AIDS Fear in Pakistan," *BBC News Online*, July 10, 2003, http://news.bbc.co.uk/1/hi/world/south_asia/3055099.stm

125. See *Illicit Drugs Situation in the Regions Neighboring Afghanistan and the Response of the ODCCP*, 28, and *Baseline Study of the Relationship between Injecting Drug Use, HIV and Hepatitis C among Male Injecting Drug Users in Lahore* (Lahore: UNDCP and UNAIDS, December 1999).

126. Ania Lichtarowicz, "Aids Fear in Pakistan," *BBC News Online*, July 10, 2003, http://news.bbc.co.uk/go/pr/fr/-/2/hi/south_asia/3055009.stm; Shahzad Raza, "Rising HIV/AIDS Cases in Pakistan: Prime Minister to Chair HIV/AIDS Meeting Today," *Daily Times* (Pakistan), November 8, 2004; "UN-Drugs-Pakistan: Risk of HIV Rises in Pakistan's Half Million Heroin Addicts," Agence France-Presse, February 26, 2003.

127. Pakistani senator, interview by authors, Islamabad, January 2005.

128. "Southwest Asia," *International Narcotics Control Strategy Report, 2003.*

129. Following several high-profile assassinations in Bombay during the 1980s, Ibrahim fled India for Dubai and resettled his family in Karachi. While he continues to move between the two cities, the August 2005 marriage of his daughter to a well-known Pakistani cricketer in Karachi attests to his family's presence in the southern port city. See Ashraf Shad, "Dawood Ibrahim Not Seen at Daughter's Wedding: Grand Show at Dubai Hotel," *Dawn*, July 25, 2005, http://www.dawn.com/2005/07/25/top13.htm, (accessed August 8, 2005); Inranil Basu, "Dawood in Karachi, But Skips Waleema," *Times of India*, August 6, 2005, http://timesofindia.indiatimes.com/articleshow/1193218.cms (accessed August 8, 2005); and "Pak Admits Dawood's Presence in Karachi," *News*, September 21, 2003, http://www.jang.com.pk/thenews/sep2003-daily/21-09-2003/main/update.shtml.

130. The authors were briefed on several of these attacks by the National Security Council Advisory Board, Delhi, September 9, 2002. For more on the Bombay blasts, see S. Hussain Zaidi, *Black Friday: The True Story of the Bombay Bomb Blasts* (New Delhi: Penguin Books India, 2003).

131. Chalk, "Non-Military Security in the Wider Middle East," 201.

132. Husain Haqqani, *Countries at the Cross-Roads: Country Profile of Pakistan* (UNPAN, 2004), http://unpan1.un.org/intradoc/groups/public/documents/NISPACee/UN AN016204.pdf.

133. See National Integrity Systems, *Transparency International Country Study Report—Pakistan 2003* (Berlin: Transparency International, 2003), 31.

134. MoI and ISI officials, interview by authors, Islamabad and Rawalpindi, January 2005. See also "Dark Days for a Black Market," *Businessweek Online*, October 15, 2001, http://www.businessweek.com/magazine/content01_42/b3753016.htm; "Iran, Pakistan Plan to Check Petroleum Smuggling: Pakistan Official," *BBC News*, December 13, 2002; "Petroleum Products Smuggling Rampant in Pakistan," *Pakistan Newswire*, April 11, 2003; "Iran-Pakistan Border Commission Discussing Border Security, Smuggling," *BBC News*, March 16, 2003; "PTA For Cut in Import Duty on Tea," *Pakistan Newswire*, May 14, 2003; Syed Aslam, "The Menace of Smuggling," *Pakistan Economist*, December 20–26, 1999.

135. Rashid, *Taliban*, 189–191; Farooq Khan, "Black Business: Smuggling Picks Up under the ATTA," *Daily Times* (Pakistan), November 18, 2004. Under the ATTA, Afghan nationals were permitted to import any good, duty free, to Pakistan; however,

these arrangements were quickly exploited by unscrupulous traders, who rapidly established markets for smuggled goods all over the country.

136. "Dark Days for a Black Market," *Businessweek Online*, October 15, 2001, http://www.businessweek.com/magazine/content01_42/b3753016.htm; Richard Behar, "Kidnapped Nation," *Fortune* 145, no. 9 (April 2002): 84; Mansoor Ahmad, "Regulations to Curb Smuggling, Under-Invoicing a Must," *Nation*, July 13, 2004.

137. Behar, "Kidnapped Nation," 84.

138. Following the crackdown on *hawala*, Pakistan's Finance Division reported that "cash remittances have averaged $356 million during the first eight months and if this trend continues, total remittances for the fiscal year 2002–03 are likely to be $4.3 billion—the highest ever in the country's history. Main factors contributing to the sharp increase in the inflow of remittances include: significant improvements in economic fundamentals, confidence of the expatriate Pakistanis in the economic management of the country; better exchange rates offered in the interbank market as against the open market; aggressive marketing of Pakistani banks in foreign countries, thereby motivating people to send their remittances through banking channels; and the crackdown on the *hundi/hawala* system in the Middle East and other parts of the world." "Pakistan's Economic Performance: During July-February, 2002–03," http://www.finance.gov.pk/summary/performance.pdf (accessed September 23, 2005).

139. FIA officials, interviews by authors, Islamabad, January 2005. See also Husain Haqqani, *Countries at the Cross-Roads*, 5, and "Pakistan Gears Up to Tackle People Smugglers," Agence France Presse, February 20, 2003. Overall, it is thought that between 100 and 150 illegal migrants cross the border in any twenty-four hour period, most of whom are women from Bangladesh and Burma who have been kidnapped or married to agents in their home countries by their parents.

140. Minimum standards—as summarized in the act—include prohibiting and punishing acts of trafficking; prescribing punishment commensurate with that for grave crimes for knowingly trafficking in its most reprehensible forms, such as for sexual purposes that involve rape, kidnapping, or death; prescribing punishment that adequately reflects the offense's heinous nature and that is sufficiently stringent to deter trafficking in any form; and undertaking to commit to serious and sustained efforts to eliminate trafficking. Modified from the U.S. State Department's *Victims of Trafficking and Violence Protection Act of 2000: Trafficking in Persons Report, 2004*, http://www.state.gov/g/tip/rls/tiprpt/2004/.

141. U.S. Department of State, *Victims of Trafficking and Violence Protection Act of 2000: Trafficking in Persons Report, 2005*, http://www.state.gov/g/tip/rls/tiprpt/2005/.

142. In 2005, fourteen states were placed in Tier 3—Bolivia, Ecuador, Qatar, the United Arab Emirates, Burma, Jamaica, Saudi Arabia, Venezuela, Cambodia, Kuwait, Sudan, Cuba, North Korea, and Togo. See U.S. Department of State, *Trafficking in Persons Report, 2005*.

143. See Ziad Haider. "Baluchis, Beijing and Pakistan's Gwadar Port," *Georgetown Journal of International Affairs* 6, no. 1 (2005).

144. Roughly 85 percent of all transactions in Pakistan are in cash, compared to just 3 percent in North America.

145. Ahmad, "Regulations to Curb Smuggling"; "Pakistan Gears Up to Tackle People Smugglers," Agence France-Presse, February 20, 2003; Behar, "Kidnapped Nation," 84; "Smuggling on Rise on GT Road, Motorway," *Pakistan Press International*, October 23, 2003.

146. "Petroleum Products Smuggling Rampant in Pakistan," *Pakistan Newswire*, April 11, 2003; "Iran, Pakistan Plan to Check Petroleum Smuggling; Pakistani Official," *BBC News*, December 13, 2003; Syed Aslam, "The Menace of Smuggling," *Pakistan Economist*, December 20–26, 1999.

147. Mumtaz Ahmad, "Cigarette Industry's Blues," *Pakistan Economist*, May 17–23, 2004.

148. "PTA for Cut in Import Duty on Tea," *Pakistan Newswire*, May 14, 2003.

149. "Smuggling on Rise on GT Road, Motorway," *Pakistan Press International*; Behar, "Kidnapped Nation," 84.

150. National Integrity Systems, *Transparency International Country Study Report— Pakistan 2003*, 31.

151. The Hudood Ordinance, for instance, which was introduced into law in 1979 under the rule of General Zia, demands that rape victims support their charge with four male Muslim witnesses, excludes the testimony of non-Muslims (and, in certain cases, women), and treats a ten-year-old female child as an adult on the basis that she has reached puberty. Such requirements have obviously greatly compounded the difficulty of establishing guilt in rape cases. See Haqqani, *Countries at the Cross-Roads*, 5; "Govt. Panel Seeks Abolition of Hudood Ordinance," *News*, September 3, 2003.

152. U.S. Department of State, *Trafficking in Persons Report, 2005*; "Pakistan Gears Up to Tackle People Smugglers," Agence France-Presse, February 20, 2003.

153. The classic definition of corruption—and the one followed by both the World Bank and Transparency International—views it as "the use of one's public position for illegitimate private gains." Although forms of corruption change from country to country, it generally includes one, some, or all of the following behaviors and practices: conflict of interest, embezzlement, fraud, bribery, political and sectarian nepotism/favoritism, and extortion. See *Global Programme Against Corruption* (Vienna: United Nations Office on Drugs and Crime, December 2004).

154. TI uses interviews and surveys to assess levels of corruption among a country's politicians and public officials. Scores of two or less in its perception index generally reflect a pervasive corruption problem that is not being met with any concerted countermeasures. In 2003, twelve countries fell into this category: Bangladesh, Nigeria, Haiti, Paraguay, Myanmar, Tajikistan, Georgia, Cameroon, Azerbaijan, Angola, Kenya,

and Tanzania. See Transparency International, "Nine Out of Ten Developing Countries Urgently Need Practical Support to Fight Corruption, Highlights New Index."

155. See, for instance, *Pakistan's Anti-Corruption Program: Observations and Recommendations* (Berlin: Transparency International, May 2002).

156. National Integrity Systems, *Transparency International Country Study Report—Pakistan 2003*, 26.

157. National Integrity Systems, *Transparency International Country Study Report—Pakistan 2003*, 8; Haqqani, *Countries at the Cross-Roads*, 7; "IMF Asks Pakistan to Reduce Corruption," *News*, October 29, 2003, http://www.jang.com.pk/thenews/oct2003-daily/29-10-2003/main/main5.htm; and Tashbih Sayyed, "Exclusive Interview: Justice (R) Sajjad Ali Shah," *Pakistan Today*, October 15, 1999, http://www.paktoday.com/shah.htm (accessed January 5, 2006). Ministry of Foreign Affairs (MFA) officials, in conversations with Fair in December 2005, objected to this sweeping characterization and noted that, in their opinion, the MFA is a positive example of an effective government agency. Consistent with this opinion, the MFA is not identified by TI as a corrupt institution.

158. See Sayyed, "Exclusive Interview: Justice (R) Sajjad Ali Shah."

159. National Integrity Systems, *Transparency International Country Study Report—Pakistan 2003*, 27.

160. See, for instance, Anatol Lieven, "The Pressures on Pakistan," *Foreign Affairs* 81, no. 1 (2002): 38; and International Centre for Peace Initiatives, *The Future of Pakistan* (Mumbai: ICPI, 2002), 79.

161. Saba Gul Khattak, Shafi ur Rehman, and Saeed Shafqat, *Perspectives on Corruption in Pakistan: A Pilot Study* (Islamabad: Sustainable Development Policy Institute, 1999), 6.

162. U.S. State Department officials, interviews by authors, Washington, D.C., November 22–23, 2004.

163. See International Commission of Jurists (ICJ), "Pakistan—Attacks on Justice 2002," August 27, 2002, http://www.icj.org/news.php3?id_article=2665&lang=en (accessed January 5, 2006). According to the ICJ, "The independence of the judiciary was largely undermined by the order by General Musharraf in January 2000 that Pakistani judges take a fresh oath of loyalty to his administration. In May 2000, the Supreme Court, reconstituted after the dismissal of six judges who refused the oath, upheld General Musharraf's military coup of 1999, under the doctrine of state necessity."

164. The government focuses much of its attention on ensuring the promotion of "suitable" chief justices, who play a key role in approving selections to the high courts, assigning cases, creating benches, and managing the electoral process. In the words of one Supreme Court advocate, recent appointees have been elevated "with the expectation that they'll toe the line. There's a distinction between looking at judicial

philosophy and looking for personal loyalty—sycophants and lackeys." Cited in ICG, *Building Judicial Independence in Pakistan*, 8. See also Mohammad Yasin and Tariq Banuri, *The Dispensation of Justice in Pakistan* (Islamabad: Oxford, 2004); Tariq Banuri, *Improving the Provision of Justice in Pakistan* (Islamabad: SDPI, 1993); Foqia Sadiq Khan and Shahrukh Rafi Khan, *A Benchmark Study on Law-And-Order and the Dispensation of Justice in the Context of Power Devolution* (Islamabad: SDPI: 2003); and "Pakistan's Fight against Corruption: Problems and Prospects," speech delivered by the chairman of the National Accountability Bureau at the International Institute for Strategic Studies, Islamabad, March 16, 2005, http://www.iiss.org/showdocument.php?docID=647 (accessed January 5, 2006).

165. ICG, *Building Judicial Independence in Pakistan*, 15.

166. Ibid., 18. According to this ICG report, members of the subordinate judiciary earn between Rs 20,000 and 40,000 ($333–666) per month, which is widely deemed inadequate for supporting a family.

167. ICG, *Building Judicial Independence in Pakistan*, 18.

168. National Integrity Systems, *Transparency International Country Study Report—Pakistan 2003*, 24.

169. Ibid., 23.

170. "Pakistan MPs Protest over Arrest," *BBC News Online*, October 31, 2003, http://news.bbc.co.uk/2/hi/south_asia/3230879.stm (accessed December 28, 2005).

171. Cited in Haqqani, *Countries at the Cross-Roads*, 7.

172. *National Accountability Ordinance, 1999, Ordinance No. XVIII of 1999, sub-section 9*; Marshuk Ali Shah, "Asian Development Bank's Anti-Corruption Initiatives," presentation given before the Conference on Combating Corruption in the Public and Private Sector, Islamabad, August 20, 2004. The groundwork for the NAB was actually laid by Nawaz Sharif as a part of his efforts to systematically vitiate the political strength of his opponent, Benazir Bhutto, and her husband, Zardari. To do so, Nawaz formed a national *ehtesab* (lit. accountability) commission through which they could be investigated on charges of corruption. The *ehtesab* commission laid the foundation for the military-appointed NAB. See Cohen, *The Idea of Pakistan*, 149.

173. The NAB's current chairman is Lieutenant General Munir Hafiz.

174. These powers include, inter alia, the right to initiate prosecutions, make arrests, transfer cases from ordinary to accountability courts, freeze property, compel banks and financial institutions to disclose documents and records, and negotiate plea bargains. See ICG, *Building Judicial Independence in Pakistan*, 24–25.

175. Figures on NAB prosecutions and investigations can be accessed via the board's official Web site at http://www.nab.gov.pk.

176. Haqqani, *Countries at the Cross-Roads*, 9–10; Ian Talbot, "General Pervez Musharraf: Savior or Destroyers of Pakistan's Democracy?" *Contemporary Southeast*

Asia 11, no. 3 (2002): 311–28; ICG, *Building Judicial Independence in Pakistan*, 25; and "Pakistan: Entire Election Deeply Flawed," *Human Rights Watch Background Briefing* (New York: Human Rights Watch, October 9, 2002).

177. See *National Anti-Corruption Strategy Report—2002* (Islamabad: National Accountability Bureau, 2002), http://www.nab.gov.pk.

178. Overall literacy rates in Pakistan currently hover around 43 percent, while net primary school enrollment for the country is only between 51 and 59 percent. See Poverty Reduction and Economic Management Sector Unit (South Asia Region), *Pakistan Development Policy Review* (New York: World Bank, April 3, 2002), 15–16.

179. National Integrity Systems, *Transparency International Country Study Report—Pakistan 2003*, 31; Haqqani, *Countries at the Cross-Road*, 4; ICG, *Building Judicial Independence in Pakistan*, 22; Asian Development Bank, *Evaluation Report for Annual Performance Review of Access to Justice Program, 2003* (Islamabad: Asian Development Bank, May 2004), 83.

180. National Integrity Systems, *Transparency International Country Study Report—Pakistan 2003*, 31.

2. U.S. Assistance Programs to Pakistan

1. FMF is often confused with Foreign Military Sales (FMS). A country can have FMS without having FMF. For example, it can buy U.S. military equipment with its own funds. While many sources cited here use the term FMS when discussing this aid, the correct term is FMF.

2. U.S. State Department officials, interviews by authors, November 2004. See also *The 9/11 Commission Report*, 367–69.

3. See "Pakistan Border Unit Gets Boost From U.S.," *Washington Post*, December 18, 2002. The equipment is part of a $73 million program to enhance Pakistan's border security. See also "Delivering Justice For The Poor In Pakistan," Asian Development Bank, News Release no. 207/01, Dec. 20, 2001, http://www.adb.org/Documents/News/2001/nr2001207.asp (accessed February 3, 2003). See also Fair, *The Counterterror Coalitions*.

4. These funds supported programs focused on child survival and health; development assistance; economic support; foreign military financing; international military education and training (IMET); international narcotics and law enforcement; and nonproliferation, antiterrorism, de-mining, and related activities. U.S. State Department officials, interviews by authors, November 2004. While this amount is substantial, it still is far less than the total allocation for Egypt, which exceeded 1.8 billion in FY 05 for the same general suite of packages. See remarks made by U.S. ambassador Nancy J. Powell, "U.S. Foreign Policy towards Pakistan," August 20, 2004, http://www.state.gov/p/sa/rls/rm/35681.htm (accessed September 28, 2005); INL, "International Narcotics and Law Enforcement: FY 2004 Budget Justification," http://www.state.gov/p/inl/rls/rpt/cbj/fy2004/21884.htm (accessed September 28, 2005). See also

Kronstadt, *Pakistan-U.S. Relations*, and Jeremy M. Sharp, *Egypt-United States Relations*, CRS Report IB93087 (Washington, D.C.: Congressional Research Service, June 15, 2005), http://www.fas.org/sgp/crs/mideast/IB93087.p (accessed October 10, 2005).

5. For details, see "Text of Draft Police D2002," published in serial form in *News* (Pakistan) on March 20, 21, 25, 28 and April 1 and 2, 2002.

6. See Peter Chalk and C. Christine Fair, "Domestic Disputes: Pakistani Internal Security," *Georgetown Journal of International Affairs* 5, no. 2 (2004).

7. *Fact Sheet: Official Working Visit of President Musharraf of Pakistan.* See also U.S. Department of State, International Information Programs, "U.S.-Pakistan Joint Group on Counter-Terrorism Meets," May 8, 2002, http://usinfo.state.gov/regiona/nea/sasia/text/0508uspak.htm.

8. See U.S. Department of State, "Media Note: Office of the Spokesman—Second Annual U.S.-Pakistan Joint Working Group on Counterterrorism and Law Enforcement," April 15, 2003, http://www.state.gov/r/pa/prs/ps/2003/19666.htm (accessed January 26, 2004). See also U.S. Department of State, "Joint Statement of the Meeting of the Pakistan-U.S. Joint Working Group on Counter-Terrorism and Law Enforcement," September 3, 2004, http://www.state.gov/p/sa/rls/pr/35966.htm (accessed July 19, 2005).

9. *The 9/11 Commission Report*, 367–369. According to this report, "If Musharraf stands for enlightened moderation in a fight for his life and for the life of his country, the United States should be willing to make hard choices too, and make the difficult long-term commitment to the future of Pakistan. Sustaining the current scale of aid to Pakistan, the United States should support Pakistan's government in its struggle against extremists with a comprehensive effort that extends from military aid to support for better education, so long as Pakistan's leaders remain willing to make difficult choices of their own."

10. U.S. State Department officials in South Asia Regional Affairs, interviews by authors, November 23, 2004.

11. U.S. Department of State, "On Overview of INL Programs in Pakistan: Combating Terrorism, Narcotics Production, and Trafficking," November 29, 2004. Provided to authors by an INL official.

12. Ibid.

13. Ibid.

14. Ibid.

15. See Office of Antiterrorism Assistance, http://www.diplomaticsecurity.org/ (accessed July 7, 2005), and testimony of U.S. ambassador Cofer Black, "Foreign Assistance and International Terrorism," April 21, 2004, http://www.state.gov/s/ct/rls/rm/2004/31672.htm (accessed July 7, 2005).

16. U.S. State Department and S/CT officials, interviews by author, November 2004.

17. Ibid.

18. See Zahid Hassan, "Al-Qaeda's New Face," *Newsline*, August 2004, 18–26. See also, Abbas, "The Pakistani Al-Qaeda," and Abbas, "What Happened."

19. See http://www.diplomaticsecurity.org/

20. Ibid.

21. Ibid.

22. U.S. State Department officials, Washington, D.C., December 2004, and FIA officials, interviews by authors, Islamabad, January 2005.

23. See USAID–Pakistan, "USAID/Pakistan Interim Strategic Plan: May 2003-September 2006," http://www.usaid.gov/pk/isp/Interim_Strategic_Plan_03_06.shtml (accessed July 7, 2005).

24. U.S. embassy, Islamabad, "USAID Provides $147 Million to Improve Pakistan's Health, Education, Economic, Governance Sectors," May 26, 2005, http://www.state.gov/p/sa/rls/pr/2005/46815.htm (accessed July 7, 2005).

25. See USAID–Pakistan, "FATA School Rehabilitation and Refurbishment," http://www.usaid.gov/pk/program_sectors/education/projects/fata_school_rehabilitation.shtml (accessed July 8, 2005).

26. In fact, ICITAP is a "subcontractor" for the INL. According to the individual who holds the Pakistan portfolio within ICITAP, each year ICITAP submits a budget to the INL. Should the INL approve the proposed project schedule, an interagency agreement is made and funds are transferred. Budget figures for ICITAP's programs in Pakistan are not publicly available, although ICITAP personnel indicate that the allocation for them is a small portion of the overall INL Pakistan budget. ICITAP personnel, in conversation with Fair, July 2005. For a description of ICITAP work in Pakistan, see "ICITAP Project Overviews for Pakistan," http://www.usdoj.gov/criminal/icitap/TextPakistan.html.

27. These include, inter alia, the FC, the ANF, the Frontier Constabulary, Customs, and the FIA.

28. See "ICITAP Project Overviews for Pakistan."

29. Ibid.

30. Ibid. Justice Department officials assert low salaries have led graft to emerge almost as an institutional practice to augment the personal incomes of police officers and to generate revenue to cover the operating expenses of the police services.

31. The comparative figure for more developed countries stands at well over 60 percent. By contrast, the majority of police in Pakistan are constables that lack the skills and expertise needed to engage in professional investigative pursuits.

32. ICITAP officials, interviews by authors, Islamabad, January 2005. See also "ICITAP Project Overviews for Pakistan."

33. ICITAP official, interview by authors, Islamabad, January 2005.

34. See "ICITAP Project Overviews for Pakistan."

35. Ibid.

36. Although global in theory, the containment strategy focuses on Pakistan, Turkey, Russia, and the Central Asian republics of Kazakhstan, Kyrgyzstan, Uzbekistan, and Tajikistan. ANF officials, interview by authors, Rawalpindi, January 2005.

37. See INL, "U.S. Government Assistance," *International Narcotics Control Strategy Report, 2005*, http://www.state.gov/g/inl/rls/nrcrpt/2005/vol1/html/42361.htm (accessed July 7, 2005).

38. See testimony of DEA administrator Karen Tandy before the U.S. House of Representatives Subcommittee on Criminal Justice, Drug Policy and Human Resources Committee on Government Reform, February 26, 2004, http://www .usdoj.gov/dea/pubs/cngrtest/ct022604.htm (accessed July 10, 2005).

39. See INL, "International Narcotics and Law Enforcement: FY 2004 Budget Justification."

40. U.S. and European officials, interviews by Fair, January 2005 and June 2005. It should be noted that at the time of this writing, Pakistan was not actively collecting fingerprints and had not made any concerted moves to link PISCES with U.S.-based databases.

41. Five Huey II helicopters and three fixed-wing surveillance aircraft were provided to the air wing based in Quetta during FY01.

42. U.S. Department of State, "On Overview of INL Programs in Pakistan: Combating Terrorism, Narcotics Production, and Trafficking," November 29, 2004. Provided to authors by an INL official.

43. Ibid.

44. Ibid.

45. Ibid.

46. This working partnership is sanctioned through an INL-ICITAP interagency agreement.

47. See "ICITAP Project Overviews for Pakistan." These programs were instituted following an ICITAP assessment of Pakistan's law enforcement capabilities first undertaken in November 2001.

48. ICITAP officials, interview by authors, Islamabad, January 2005.

49. Such efforts take place at the National Police Academy in Rawalpindi and the Police College Sahala in Sindh and are focused on building management skills, augmenting internal training capacity, and heightening overall investigative expertise.

50. See "ICITAP Project Overviews for Pakistan." The MoI and the National Police Management are responsible for establishing a national vision and focus for future consultations in these and other areas.

51. This course is intended to build core competencies in a variety of areas among fixed-border-position police personnel who are deemed critical to Pakistan's entry and border-post operations. See "ICITAP Project Overviews for Pakistan."

52. Key topics covered in this course include basic crime-scene investigation techniques, evidence collection and processing, and crime-scene reconstruction. See "ICITAP Project Overviews for Pakistan."

53. This series of seminars focuses on building organizational capacity and sustainability and use of force decision making. See http://www.usdoj.gov/criminal/icitap/TextPakistan.html.

54. These laboratories are located in Lahore, Karachi, Peshawar, Quetta, and Rawalpindi.

55. Projected costs for developing these areas is expected to be in the $4 million range. Notably, ICITAP is not currently helping to build any sort of DNA analysis capacity in Pakistan.

56. ICITAP official, interview by authors, Islamabad, January 2005.

57. Ibid.

58. The fundamental operations of AFIS are relatively straightforward and include taking and scanning fingerprints, capturing facial images, entering personal data, and cross-referencing this information with information uploaded from the FIA mainframe.

59. ICITAP official, interview by authors, Islamabad, January 2005. At the time of writing only two remote terminals were up and running—one in Islamabad and one in Lahore.

60. Ibid.

61. Ibid.

62. One of this study's authors has training in biological sciences and does not agree with this assertion. The fundamental principles of DNA analysis remain largely the same even if the technological means continue to develop.

63. Officials at police headquarters, interview by Fair, Islamabad, January 2005.

64. See INL, "U.S. Government Assistance," *International Narcotics Control Strategy Report 2005.*

65. The United States has no specific programs to counter the smuggling of goods.

66. See Office to Monitor and Combat Trafficking in Persons, "The U.S. Government's International Anti-Trafficking Programs," June 3, 2005, http://www.state.gov/g/tip/rls/rpt/47201.htm.

67. See "Pakistan—Newly Established Anti-Trafficking Unit Receives IOM Training," IOM Press Briefing Notes, May 17, 2005. See also IOM, *Data and Research on Human Trafficking: A Global Survey* (Geneva: IOM, 2005), http://www.iom.int/iomwebsite/Publication/ServletSearchPublication?event=detail&id=4351# (accessed August 22, 2005).

68. Office to Monitor and Combat Trafficking in Persons, "The U.S. Government's International Anti-Trafficking Programs."

69. Although Pakistan introduced in 2002 an ordinance dealing with the control of human trafficking, it had, at the time of this writing, yet to implement the legislation. See UN Office for the Coordination of Humanitarian Affairs, "Pakistan: IOM Launches Counter Trafficking Course," July 27, 2004.

70. See Paul Simons, deputy assistant secretary of state for economic and business affairs, before the HIRC Subcommittee on International Terrorism and Nonproliferation and House Financial Services Subcommittee on Oversight and Investigations, "Starving Terrorists of Money: The Role of the Middle East Financial Institutions," May 4, 2005, http://wwwc.house.gov/international_relations/109/sim050405.pdf (accessed July 14, 2005). See also Anthony Wayne, assistant secretary of state for economic and business affairs, testimony to the House Committee on International Relations, Subcommittee on International Terrorism, Nonproliferation and Human Rights, March 26, 2003, http://www.state.gov/e/eb/rls/rm/2003/19113.htm, accessed July 10, 2005.

71. S/CT officials, interview by authors, November 2004. See also INL, "Bilateral Activities," *International Narcotics Control Strategy Report, 2005*, http://www.state.gov/g/inl/rls/nrcrpt/2005/vol2/html/42384.htm (accessed July 7, 2005); and Simons, "Starving Terrorists of Money: The Role of the Middle East Financial Institutions."

72. Among the key benchmarks are those established by the Financial Action Task Force (FATF), a thirty-three-member international body formed to promulgate international anti-money laundering and counterterrorist financing standards. For more information, see http://www1.oecd.org/fatf/40Recs_en.htm (accessed on July 14, 2005). See also Maurice R. Greenberg and Mallory Factor, *Update on the Global Campaign Against Terrorist Financing: Second Report of an Independent Task Force on Terrorist Financing Sponsored by the Council on Foreign Relations*, June 15, 2004, http://www.cfr.org/pdf/Revised_Terrorist_Financing.pdf (accessed July 14, 2005).

73. U.S. State Department official, interview by authors, Washington, D.C., November 2004. It should also be noted that Pakistan's failure to sign the UN Convention for the Suppression of the Financing of Terrorism has also negatively impacted on the

United States' willingness and latitude to provide Islamabad with more definitive assistance and training to crack down on terrorist financing.

74. See the program description for these USAID–Pakistan efforts at "Democracy and Governance: Background," http://www.usaid.gov/pk/governance/ (accessed July 14, 2005). See also Nancy J. Powell. "U.S. Foreign Policy Towards Pakistan," November 13, 2003, http://www.state.gov/p/sa/rls/rm/26277.htm (accessed July 14, 2005). In FY05, USAID funding totaled more than $13 million. USAID is also supporting Pakistan's devolution process, which is discussed in chapter 3.

75. See "USAID Pakistan Program Data Sheet 391-004," http://www.usaid.gov/pubs/cbj2003/ane/pk/391-004.html (accessed August 22, 2005).

76. See USAID, "Budget Justification to the Congress: Fiscal Year 2006," http://www.usaid.gov/policy/budget/cbj2006/ane/pk.html (accessed July 14, 2005).

77. TI–P staff, in personal communication with Fair, July 2005. See also TI–P, "About TI-Pakistan," http://www.transparency.org.pk/org/abouttipak.htm (accessed July 14, 2005), and USAID, "Pakistan Data Sheet: Democracy and Governance, FY 2004," http://www.usaid.gov/our_work/democracy_and_governance/regions/ane/pakistan.pdf (accessed July 14, 2005).

78. This stands in contrast to TI–Bangladesh, where far more concerted action is being taken to tackle the problem of corruption.

3. Assessment of U.S. Assistance

1. MoI and FIA officials, interview by authors, Islamabad, January 2005.

2. U.S. State Department officials, interview by authors, Washington, D.C., November 2004.

3. Ibid.

4. U.S. officials, interviews by authors, Washington, D.C., and Islamabad, November 2004 and January 2005.

5. U.S. and Pakistani officials, interviews by authors, Islamabad, January 2005. And author observations.

6. Akhatar Marawat, MoI, interview by authors, Islamabad, January 2005.

7. U.S. State Department officials, interviews by authors, Washington, D.C., November 2004, and Pakistani officials, interviews by authors, January 2005.

8. U.S. State Department officials, interviews by authors, Washington, D.C., November 2004. The alternative, of course, is that the bulk of training be done in Pakistan. There are two principal drawbacks to this. First, recipients of this aid see going to the United States as a sign of respect. Second, bringing such persons and the needed equipment to Pakistan is costly and leaves a large footprint, which is not desirable under prevailing security conditions.

9. U.S. State Department officials, interviews by authors, Washington, D.C., November 2004. U.S. officials purport to be working actively with their Pakistani counterparts to avoid such inefficient uses of human capital investment.

10. U.S. State Department officials, interviews by authors, Washington, D.C., November 2004. See also INL, "Bilateral Activities," *International Narcotics Control Strategy Report 2005*; and Simons, "Starving Terrorists of Money: The Role of the Middle East Financial Institutions," http://www.house.gov/international_relations/109/sim050405.pdf.

11. U.S. State Department officials, interviews by authors, Washington, D.C., November 2004. Pakistan has enacted specific money-laundering provisions, which are contained under Articles 11J and 11K of the country's (1987) Anti-Terrorism Act. However, these provisions are not considered to be of a standard that meets FATF requirements.

12. U.S. State Department officials, interviews by authors, Washington, D.C., and Pakistani officials, interview by authors, Islamabad, October 2004–June 2005. It should be noted that the new port planned for Gwadar in Baluchistan is being considered as a possible candidate for container-security assistance. The thinking (and hope) in U.S. and Pakistani government circles is that this will help to provide the country with a safer, more efficient, and less corrupt alternative maritime hub to the traditionally problematic facility at Karachi.

13. "ICITAP Project Overviews for Pakistan."

14. Ibid.

15. Various Pakistani officials, interviews by authors, Islamabad, January 2005.

16. The government often cites an ostensible lack of evidence to prosecute a case. Skeptics note, however, that lack of evidentiary standards has certainly not deterred the state from detaining and imprisoning other persons deemed to be a threat to the ruling administration (consider, for example, the 2003 arrest of Javed Hashmi). This view was aired by U.S. State Department officials in interviews conducted in 2002 and was repeatedly shared by Pakistanis during Fair's in-country research trips in August 2003, February 2004, and January 2005.

17. Despite numerous Pakistani proclamations about *madrassah* registration initiatives and *madrassah* reforms, these efforts have not been successful. As noted in chapter 1, in the most recent installation of this saga, another "breakthrough" has recently been heralded. Under the new deal, *madaris* no longer have to reveal the sources of their funding. However, the seminaries are threatening to sabotage even this deal if other concessions are not given by the government. Given that one of the primary reasons for requiring *madrassah* registration was to obtain information about foreign and other funding, this concession is flabbergasting. See Abbas, "Pakistan Madrassa Row 'Resolved'"; "Govt-ITMD Deal Is Not Good Enough," *Friday Times* (Pakistan), September 25, 2005, http://www.dailytimes.com.pk/default.asp?page=story_25-9-2005_pg3_1 (accessed September 28, 2005); Mohammad Imran, "Madrassas Don't

Need to Give Details of Donors," *Friday Times*, September 25, 2005, http://www
.dailytimes.com.pk/default.asp?page=story_24-9-2005_pg1_1 (accessed September
28, 2005). See also Zulfikar Ali, "Back to Camp," *Herald* (Pakistan), July 2005; Zaffar
Abbas, "Operation Eyewash," *Herald* (Pakistan), August 2005; Syed Shoaib Hasan,
"The Untouchables," *Herald* (Pakistan), August 2005; and Syed Shoaib Hasan,
"Keeping Secrets," *Herald* (Pakistan), August 2005.

18. U.S. officials, interviews with authors, Washington, D.C., November 2004 and
Islamabad, January 2005. Then U.S. ambassador to Afghanistan, Zalmay Khalilzad,
vexed Pakistani officials by making precisely this allegation, one that Islamabad
vociferously rejected. U.S. military personnel, meanwhile, are of the belief that militants
operating against U.S. and coalition forces in Afghanistan are being aided by the Frontier
Constabulary, which reportedly provides the militants information about troop
positions and movements. U.S. military officials in Pakistan, in discussion with Fair,
September 2005. For a reference to Khalilzad's comments, see "Pakistan Extends
Qaeda Deadline, *CBS News Online*, April 19, 2004, http://www.cbsnews.com/stories/
2004/04/21/terror/main612988.shtml. For a Pakistani account of Islamabad's supposed inaction against militants engaging in cross border attacks on U.S. and coalition
forces, see M. Ilyas Khan, "Who Are These People," *Herald* (Pakistan), April 2004.

19. Senator Mushahid Hussain and Pervaiz Iqbal Cheema, interviews on *Radio Aap ki
Duniya*, August 31, 2005, http://www.voanews.com/aapkidunyaa/ (accessed September 6, 2005).

20. Fair, "Militant Recruitment in Pakistan"; Rana, *The A to Z of Jehadi Groups in
Pakistan*.

21. See Zulfikar Ali, "Back to Camp," *Herald* (Pakistan), July 2005; Abbas, "Operation
Eyewash."

22. Indicative of the double standards that Islamabad appears to exhibit in terms of
countering Islamist militancy in Pakistan was President Musharraf's July 15, 2005,
pledge to institute a comprehensive crackdown on all extremist elements in the
country. Notably, however, subsequent instructions from the MoI specified that only
mosques, *madaris*, and radicals connected with sectarian groups should be targeted,
which by default, insulated Kashmiri *tanzeems* (and, arguably, foreign elements) from
the dragnet. For further details, see Syed Shoaib Hasan, "The Untouchables," *Herald*
(Pakistan), August 2005.

23. FIA officials, in conversation with the authors, Islamabad, January 2005.

24. Reform was essential. Prior to 2002, Pakistan based its policing on a nineteenth-
century British colonial framework, which itself was modeled on the Irish constabulary
and not suited to serving the civilian needs of a modern, sovereign, independent state.
When Musharraf assumed power in 1999, he established the National Reconstruction
Bureau (NRB) to initiate high-level reform in several of the country's important
institutional structures, including the police forces. The culmination of various multi-
agency efforts to establish a new policing system was the PO, which draws heavily on
contemporary modalities employed in Japan and Great Britain. Retired and serving

police officials, interviews by authors, Islamabad, January 2004. See also *Police Order, 2002 [Chief Executive's Order No. 22 of 2002, dated 14.8.02]* (Lahore: National Law Book House, 2002) and Afzal Shigri, "Implementing Police Order 2002: A Dilemma for the Provinces," *News* (Pakistan), November 8, 2003.

25. This aspect of the PO was viewed as especially significant, not least because police in Pakistan have tended to act as the hired "henchmen" of prevailing political leaders or important local figures and families. See Afzal Shigri, "Implementing Police Order 2002: A Dilemma for the Provinces," *News* (Pakistan), November 8, 2003; and his "Policing the Police," *News* (Pakistan), April 10, 2004.

26. *Police Order, 2002 (Order 22 of 2002) As Amended [sic] by the Police Order (Amendment) Ordinance (V of 2002)* (Lahore: Manzoor Law Book House, 2005); Afzal A. Shigri, "Institutionalizing Political Interference in Policing," *News* (Pakistan), December 8, 2004.

27. See testimony by Assistant Secretary Christina Rocca before the U.S. House of Representatives Committee on International Relations, given June 22, 2004, "United States Interests and Foreign Policy Priorities in South Asia," http://wwwc.house.gov/international_relations/108/roc062204.htm.

28. Pakistan embassy officials, interviews by authors, Washington, D.C., June 2005.

29. Both the PPP and the PML have been barred from participating in national elections since Musharraf's assumption of power in 1999. This is justified on the grounds that Pakistan's civilian political leaders were both corrupt and inept. For a critique of this devolution plan, see International Crisis Group, *Devolution in Pakistan: Reform or Regression?* Asia Report, no. 77 (Brussels/Islamabad: ICG, March 22, 2004).

30. Current and serving Pakistani police officials and independent scholars, in conversation with the authors, Islamabad, January 2005, and with Fair, June 2005.

31. This policy stance has been repeatedly emphasized by the Bush administration in the years since 9/11.

32. Fair fieldwork in 2003 and 2004 and Fair and Chalk fieldwork in 2005. This issue is also addressed at length in Fair, "Islam and Politics in Pakistan," and C. Christine Fair and Karthik Vaidyanathan, "The Practice of Islam in Pakistan and Islam's Influence on Pakistani Politics," in Prospects for Peace in South Asia, ed. Rafiq Dossani and Henry Rowen (Palo Alto, Calif.: Stanford University Press, 2005).

33. For an extensive account of this involvement, see Rana, *The A to Z of Jehadi Organizations in Pakistan*. According to Dennis Kux, "Although Pakistan did not begin the [1989] uprising in Kashmir, the temptation to fan the flames was too great for Islamabad to resist. Using guerrilla-warfare expertise gained during the Afghan war, Pakistan's ISI began to provide active backing for Kashmiri Muslim insurgents." Dennis Kux, *The United States and Pakistan 1947–2000: Disenchanted Allies* (Washington: Woodrow Wilson Center Press, 2001), 305. See also Alexander Evans, "The Kashmir Insurgency: As Bad as It Gets," *Small Wars and Insurgencies* 11, no. 1 (2000) and Kronstadt, *International Terrorism in South Asia*, Congressional Research Service Report

RS21658 (Washington, D.C.: Congressional Research Service, November 3, 2003). For a critique of the Pakistan Army's role in the ongoing sanguineous violence in Kashmir, see Selig S. Harrison, "Peace and Human Rights in Kashmir," testimony prepared for the Subcommittee on Human Rights and Wellness, Committee on Government Reform, U.S. House of Representatives, May 12, 2004, http://reform.house.gov/UploadedFiles/House%20Testimony%20of%20Selig%20Harrison.pdf.

34. Harrison, "Peace and Human Rights in Kashmir."

35. This point of view was aired by a wide array of analysts, journalists, and retired military officers to Fair during her trips to Pakistan in 2003, 2004, and 2005. Numerous Pakistani officials and journalists have expressed similar sentiments to Fair while visiting the United States. Even members of the MMA have been vocal in terms of this issue, explicitly chastising President Musharraf's notions of democracy during a July 2005 meeting at the Brookings Institution in Washington, D.C.

36. For more information on this poll, see Pew Research Center, "U.S. Image Up Slightly, But Still Negative American Character Gets Mixed Reviews," June 2005, http://pewglobal.org/reports/display.php?ReportID=247.

37. For more on the utility of socioeconomic tools as part of a broader counterterrorist strategy, see Kim Craigin and Peter Chalk, *Terrorism and Development: Using Social and Economic Development to Inhibit a Resurgence of Terrorism* (Santa Monica, Calif.: RAND, 2003).

38. MoI and Ministry of Foreign Affairs officials, interviews by authors, Islamabad, January 2005.

39. It should be noted that U.S. officials justify this decision not so much on counter-terrorism grounds but on the need to ensure that the air wing will not be commandeered by the military and misused for purposes that either have no practical strategic benefit, such as VIP transportation, or that are at odds with U.S. geopolitical objectives, such as carrying surveillance over the Indian-Pakistan border, which would generate considerable consternation in Delhi. U.S. embassy officials, interviews by authors, Islamabad, January 2005.

40. MoI and Ministry of Foreign Affairs officials, interviews by authors, Islamabad, January 2005. Officials in Pakistan also pointed out a number of logistical problems with the air wing, namely, that because most equipment comes from the United States, the maintenance trail is both inefficient and excessively long. Further, there is a general lack of basic maintenance infrastructure on the ground, such as aircraft hangars and a proper workshop.

41. Apart from creating problems in adequately assessing the utility of U.S. assistance, Washington's marginal presence in Pakistan may, in fact, be contributing to ongoing perceptions about the country's adverse threat environment—precisely because so few government personnel are able to travel outside the capital.

42. U.S. State Department officials, interview by authors, Washington, D.C., November 2004.

43. It should be noted that in some cases the United States has attempted to work with Pakistan to overcome the language barrier. At the Sahala Police Academy, for example, bilingual instructors are available and all print and audio materials are left with the commandant so that they can be translated into Urdu for subsequent internal use. MoI, FIA, and Pakistani police officials, interviews by authors, Islamabad, January 2005.

44. U.S. State Department officials, interviews by authors, January 2005.

45. See the discussion of U.S. options in Cohen, *The Idea of Pakistan*, 301–329.

46. ANF officials, interviews by authors, Rawalpindi, Islamabad, January 2005.

47. According to the ANF, the United States is planning on earmarking some $780 million to support counternarcotics activities in Afghanistan (compared to an annual allocation of only $0.7 million to Pakistan). Most of this money will be invested in the Counter-Narcotics Directorate (CND) and Counter-Narcotics Police Agency (CNPA), highly nascent organizations whose effectiveness has yet to be proven. Officials also point out that there is, as yet, no standardized system of criminal penalization for drugs in Afghanistan, meaning that there is no legal recourse for taking the law to its final conclusions in narcotics cases.

48. By contrast, the ANF lauds Great Britain's approach to counternarcotics, which in the opinion of one senior official is more complex, multidimensional, and long-term in nature. The British currently take the lead in instituting drug assistance to Pakistan, remaining particularly active in Baluchistan, where more than £1 million has been made available in funding.

49. While the United States has provided training and communications equipment to the Frontier Corps, no explicit package of support has been made available. The ANF believes this is a serious void, not least because it is impossible for the Pakistani state to institute a concerted counternarcotics program in the tribal areas without the support of the corps.

50. U.S. defense officials, in conversation with the authors, Islamabad, September 2005.

Postscript

1. The disaster triggered an outpouring of international relief assistance, with the United States making an initial pledge of $156 million (roughly Rs 3 billion) in emergency aid.

2. Indeed, there was early speculation that the seismic events of October 8 could serve to actually topple the regime.

3. For JuD's own coverage of its activities, see its Web site, http://www.jamatuddawa. org/English2/index.htm (accessed December 30, 2005); See also Syed Shoib Hasan and Intikhab Amir, "The New Fault Line," *Herald* (Pakistan), November 2005, 55–57; Intikhab Amir, "Rediscovering Militants: International Organisations Look towards Militants-Turned-Volunteers for Credible Relief Delivery," *Herald* (Pakistan), Decem-

ber 2005, 84–87; Dan McDougall, "Government's Earthquake Aid Failure Fuels Calls for Holy War," *Scotsman*, October 16, 2005, http://www.jamatuddawa.org/ English2/news/200510/19/failure.htm (accessed December 30, 2005);Carlotta Gall and Arif Jamal, "In a Remote Camp, Help from an Unconventional Source," *New York Times*, October 18, 2005; Declan Walsh, "Pakistani Extremists Take Lead on Earthquake Disaster Aid: International Relief Agencies Are Only Beginning to Arrive," *San Francisco Chronicle*, October 17, 2005; Declan Welsh, "Extremist Measures: An Islamic Aid Group is Proving to Be One of the Most Popular Relief Providers in Quake-Hit Kashmir," *Guardian* (UK), October 18, 2005; Stephen Ulph, "Jihadists Respond to Earthquake Victims in Pakistan," *Terrorism Focus* 2, no. 20 (2005); Steve Coll, "After the Earthquake, Some Strange New Alliances," *New Yorker*, November 21, 2005, http://www.newyorker.com/printables/fact/051121fa_fact (accessed December 30, 2005); and Joseph R. Biden, "Floor Statement: Earthquake Relief for Pakistan," October 25, 2005, http://biden.senate.gov/newsroom/details.cfm?id=249256&& (accessed December 30, 2005).

Bibliography

Abbas, Zaffar. "Pakistan Madrassa Row 'Resolved.'" *BBC News Online*, September 25, 2005. http://news.bbc.co.uk/2/hi/south_asia/4275848.stm (accessed September 28, 2005).

———. "Operation Eyewash." *Herald* (Pakistan), August 2005.

———. "Pakistan's Military-Militant Link." *BBC News Online*, June 16, 2005. http://news.bbc.co.uk/go/pr/fr/-/world/south_asia/4094716.stm.

———. "The Fifth Column." *Herald* (Pakistan), June 2005.

———. "What Happened." *Herald* (Pakistan), June 2005.

———. "The Pakistani Al-Qaeda." *Herald* (Pakistan), August 2004.

Ahmad, Mansoor. "Regulations to Curb Smuggling, Under-Invoicing a Must." *Nation*, July 13, 2004.

Ahmad, Mumtaz. "Cigarette Industry's Blues." *Pakistan Economist*, May 17–23, 2004.

———. "What Happened." *Herald* (Pakistan), June 2005. "Islam and the States: The Case of Pakistan." In *Religious Challenge to the State*, edited by Matthew Moen and L. Gustafson. Philadelphia: Temple University Press, 1992.

Ahmed, Akbar S. *Order and Conflict in Waziristan: Religion and Politics in an Islamic Society.* Cambridge: Cambridge University Press, 1983. Reprinted 2004.

Ahmed, Khaled. "Debate on Textbooks, Pakistani Style." *Friday Times*, April 16, 2004.

Alam, Sara. "The Rising Toll of Drug Addicts." *Spiros Tzelepis*, July-August 2002. http://users.otenet.gr/~tzelepisk/yc/24.htm.

Ali, Zulfiqar. "Back to the Camps." *Herald* (Pakistan), July 2005.

Amir, Intikhab. "Rediscovering Militants: International Organisations Look Towards Militants-Turned-Volunteers for Credible Relief Delivery." *Herald* (Pakistan), December 2005, 84–87.

Amnesty International, "Human Rights Abuses in the Search for al-Qa'ida and Taliban in the Tribal Areas," April 1, 2004. http://web.amnesty .org/library/index/engasa330112004 (accessed September 23, 2005).

Andrabi, Tahir et al. "Religious School Enrollment in Pakistan: A Look at the Data." Working Paper, World Bank, February 2005. http://econ .worldbank.org/external/default/main?pagePK=64165259&piPK= 64165421&menuPK=64166093&theSitePK=469372&entityID=00 0112742_20050228152509/ (accessed October 3, 2005).

"Another Provocation." *Economist*, January 26, 2002.

Asian Development Bank, "Pakistan: Economic Update (July 2004-March 2005)." http://www.adb.org/Documents/Economic_Updates/ PAK/default.asp (accessed August 22, 2005).

Aslam, Syed. "The Menace of Smuggling." *Pakistan Economist*, December 20–26, 1999.

Banuri, Tariq. *Improving the Provision of Justice in Pakistan* (Islamabad: SDPI, 1993).

Baseline Study of the Relationship Between Injecting Drug Use, HIV and Hepatitis C Among Male Injecting Drug Users in Lahore. Lahore: UNDCP and UNAIDS, 1999.

Basrur, Rajesh. "Coercive Diplomacy in a Nuclear Environment." Prospects for Peace in South Asia: 2nd Conference on South Asian Security, Bechtel Conference Center, Stanford University, January 2003.

Basu, Inranil. "Dawood in Karachi, But Skips Waleema." *Times of India*, August 6, 2005. http://timesofindia.indiatimes.com/articleshow/ 1193218.cms (accessed August 8, 2005).

Behar, Richard. "Kidnapped Nation." *Fortune* 145, no. 9 (April 2002).

Biden, Joseph R. "Floor Statement: Earthquake Relief for Pakistan." October 25, 2005. http://biden.senate.gov/newsroom/details.cfm? id=249256&& (accessed December 30, 2005).

Black, Cofer. "Foreign Assistance and International Terrorism." Prepared for the Senate Appropriations Subcommittee on Foreign Operations.

April 21, 2004. http://www.state.gov/s/ct/rls/rm/2004/31672 .htm (accessed July 7, 2005).

Blanche, Ed. "Iran Struggles With Narcotics Scourge." *Jane's Intelligence Review* (October 2000).

Blank, Jonah. "Kashmir-Fundamentalism Takes Root." *Foreign Affairs* 78, no. 6 (1999).

Blood, Peter. *Pakistan-US Relations.* Washington, D.C.: Congressional Research Service, February 12, 2002.

Bose, Sumantra. *The Challenge in Kashmir: Democracy, Self-Determination and a Just Peace.* New Delhi: Sage Books, 1997.

British Security Service JTAC. Interview by author. London, January 2005.

Chalk, Peter. "Non-Military Security in the Wider Middle East." *Studies in Conflict and Terrorism* 26, no. 3 (2003).

———. *Non-Military Security and Global Order: The Impact of Violence, Chaos and Extremism on National and International Security.* London: Macmillan, 2000.

Chalk, Peter and C. Christine Fair. "United States Law Enforcement Assistance to Pakistan." In *Civilian Security Assistance, Democracy and Human Rights*, edited by Olga Oliker et al. Santa Monica, Calif.: RAND, forthcoming.

———. "Domestic Disputes: Pakistani Internal Security." *Georgetown Journal of International Affairs* 5, no. 2 (2004).

Chanrasekaran, Rajiv and Rama Lakshmi. "New Delhi Lays Blame." *Washington Post*, December 29, 2001.

Cheema, Pervaiz Iqbal and Senator Mushahid Hussain. Panel dicussion including C. Fair, Hussain Haqqani and Samina Ahmed. August 31, 2005. http://www.voanews.com/aapkidunyaa/ (accessed September 6, 2005).

Chopra, V.D., ed. *Rise of Terrorism and Secessionism in Eurasia.* New Delhi: Gyan Publishing House, 2001.

Chouvy, Pierre-Arnaud. "Afghan Opium Production Predicted to Reach New High." *Jane's Intelligence Review* (October 2004).

Cohen, Stephen P. *Idea of Pakistan*. Washington, D.C.: Brookings Institution Press, 2004.

Coll, Steve. "After the Earthquake, Some Strange New Alliances." *New Yorker*, November 21, 2005. http://www.newyorker.com/printables/fact/051121fa_fact (accessed December 30, 2005).

———. *Ghost Wars: The Secret History of the CIA, Afghanistan, and Bin Laden, from the Soviet Invasion to September 10, 2001*. New York: Penguin, 2004.

Coulson, N.J. *A History of Islamic Law*. Edinburgh: Edinburgh University Press, 1964.

Cowell, Alan and Don Van Natta. "4 From Britain Carried Out Terror Blasts, Police Say." *New York Times*, July 13, 2005.

Craigin, Kim and Peter Chalk. *Terrorism and Development. Using Social and Economic Development to Inhibit a Resurgence of Terrorism*. Santa Monica, Calif.: RAND, 2003.

"Dark Days for a Black Market." *Businessweek Online*, October 15, 2001. http://www.businessweek.com/magazine/content01_42/b3753016.htm.

"Delivering Justice For The Poor In Pakistan." Asian Development Bank, News Release no. 207/01, December 20, 2001. http://www.adb.org/Documents/News/2001/nr2001207.asp (accessed February 3, 2003).

"Dozens Killed in Pakistan Blast." *BBC News Online*, October 7, 2004. http://newsvote.bbc.co.uk.

Dugger, Celia and Barry Bearak. "Indian Officials Tie Attack to a Pakistani-Based Group, But the FBI Chief Demurs." *New York Times*, January 23, 2002.

"Editorial: Retreating on the Madrassas." *Daily Times* (Pakistan), August 5, 2002.

"Eleven Killed in Karachi Attack." *BBC News Online*, June 10, 2004. http://newsvote.bbc.co.uk.

Embassy of Pakistan officials. Interviews by author. Washington, D.C., June 2005.

Evans, Alexander. "The Kashmir Insurgency: As Bad As It Gets." *Small Wars and Insurgencies* 11, no.1 (2000).

"Extremist Measures: An Islamic Aid Group Is Proving To Be One of the Most Popular Relief Providers in Quake-Hit Kashmir, Writes Declan Walsh." *Guardian* (UK), October 18, 2005.

"Eyeball to Eyeball." *Economist*, January 5, 2002.

Fact Sheet: Official Working Visit of President Musharraf of Pakistan, US Programs to Assist the People of Pakistan, February 13, 2002. http://www.whitehouse.gov/news/releases/2002/02/20020213-10.html (accessed August 30, 2005).

Fair, C. Christine. *The Counterterror Coalitions: Cooperation with Pakistan and India.* Santa Monica, Calif.: RAND, 2004.

———. "Militant Recruitment in Pakistan." *Studies in Conflict and Terrorism* 27, no. 6 (2004).

———. "Islam and Politics in Pakistan." In *The Muslim World and the United States After 9/11 and the Iraq War*, edited by Angel Rabasa (Santa Monica, Calif.: RAND, 2004).

Fair, C. Christine, Karthik Vaidyanathan, Rafiq Dossani, and Henry Rowen, eds. *Prospects for Peace in South Asia.* Palo Alto, Calif.: Stanford University Press, 2005.

Foster, Peter and Nasir Malick. "Suicide Bombers Flew to Pakistan Together." *Daily Telegraph* (UK), July 19, 2005.

Gall, Carlotta and Arif Jamal. "In a Remote Camp, Help From an Unconventional Source." *New York Times*, October 18, 2005.

Ganguly, Summit. *The Crisis in Kashmir.* Washington, D.C.: Woodrow Wilson Center Press, 1997.

Global Programme Against Corruption. Vienna: United Nations Office on Drugs and Crime, 2004.

Government of India, Ministry of External Affairs. "Statement on Telephone Call by US Secretary of State and on Visit of US Deputy Secretary of State Richard Armitage," June 8, 2002. http://meaindia.nic.in/event/2002/06/08event01.htm (accessed October 8, 2005).

Government of Pakistan, Finance Division. "Pakistan's Economic Performance: During July-February, 2002-03." http://www.finance.gov
.pk/summary/performance.pdf (accessed September 23, 2005).

"Govt-ITMD Deal Is Not Good Enough." *Friday Times,* September 25, 2005. http://www.dailytimes.com.pk/default.asp?page=story_25-9-2005_pg3_1 (accessed September 28, 2005).

Grare, Frédéric. *Pakistan: The Resurgence of Baluch Nationalism.* Carnegie Papers, no. 65. Washington, D.C.: Carnegie Endowment for International Peace, January 2006. http://www.carnegieendowment.org/files/CP65.Grare.FINAL.pdf (accessed January 30, 2006).

Greenberg, Maurice R. and Mallory Factor. *Update on the Global Campaign Against Terrorist Financing: Second Report of an Independent Task Force on Terrorist Financing Sponsored by the Council on Foreign Relations,* June 15, 2004. http://www.cfr.org/pdf/Revised_Terrorist_Financing.pdf (accessed July 14, 2005).

Haider, Ziad. "Baluchis, Beijing and Pakistan's Gwadar Port." *Georgetown Journal of International Affairs* 6, no. 1 (2005).

Haqqani, Husain. *Pakistan: Between Mosque and Military.* Washington D.C.: CEIP, 2005.

————. *Countries at the Cross-Roads: Country Profile of Pakistan, 2004.* UNPAN, 2004. http://unpan1.un.org/intradoc/groups/public/documents/nispacee/unpan016204.pdf (accessed September 6, 2005).

Harding, Luke and Rosie Cowan. "Pakistan Militants Linked to London Attacks." *Guardian* (UK), July 19, 2005.

Hasan, Khalid. "Major Terror Figure Arrested in Karachi, Flown Out to U.S." *Daily Times* (Pakistan), May 9, 2002.

Hasan, Syed Shoaib. "Keeping Secrets." *Herald* (Pakistan), August 2005.

————. "The Untouchables." *Herald* (Pakistan), August 2005.

Hasan, Syed Shoaib and Intikhab Amir. "The New Fault Line." *Herald* (Pakistan), November 2005.

Hassan, Zahid. "Al-Qaeda's New Face." *Newsline,* August 2004.

Horowitz, Donald. *Ethnic Groups in Conflict*. Berkeley: University of California Press, 1985.

Howard, Roger. "Probing the Ties that Bind Militant Islam." *Jane's Intelligence Review* (February 2000).

Howard, Shaun. "The Afghan Connection: Islamic Extremism in Central Asia." *National Security Studies Quarterly* (Summer 2000).

IB and National Security Council Advisory Board. Interview by authors. Delhi, September 2002.

Illicit Drugs Situation in the Regions Neighboring Afghanistan and the Response of the ODCCP. Vienna: United Nations Office for Drug Control and Crime Prevention, October 2002.

"IMF Asks Pakistan to Reduce Corruption." *News*, October 29, 2003. http://www.jang.com.pk/thenews/oct2003-daily/29-10-2003/main/main5.htm.

"Implementing Police Order 2002: A Dilemma for the Provinces." *News*, November 8, 2003.

Imran, Mohammad. "Madrassas Don't Need to Give Details of Donors." *Friday Times*, September 25, 2005. http://www.dailytimes.com.pk/default.asp?page=story_24-9-2005_pg1_1 (accessed September 28, 2005).

International Centre for Peace Initiatives. *The Future of Pakistan*. Mumbai: ICPI, 2002.

International Commission of Jurists. "Pakistan—Attacks on Justice 2002," August 27, 2002. http://www.icj.org/news.php3?id_article=2665&lang=en (last accessed January 5, 2006).

International Crisis Group. *Building Judicial Independence in Pakistan*. ICG Asia Report, no. 86. Islamabad/Brussels: ICG, 2004.

———. *Devolution in Pakistan: Reform or Regression?* ICG Asia Report, no. 77. Islamabad/Brussels: ICG, 2004.

———. *Pakistan: Madrassahs, Extremism and the Military*. ICG Asia Report, no. 36. Islamabad/Brussels: ICG, 2002.

International Organization for Migration. *Data and Research on Human Trafficking: A Global Survey.* Geneva: IOM, 2005. http://www.iom .int/iomwebsite/Publication/ServletSearchPublication?event= detail&id=4351# (accessed August 22, 2005).

Inter-Services Intelligence Directorate and Ministry of the Interior. Interview by authors. Rawalpindi and Islamabad, January 2005.

"Interview with Major General Shaukat Sultan." *Herald*, November 2005.

"Iran-Pakistan Border Commission Discussing Border Security, Smuggling." *BBC News*, March 16, 2003.

"Iran, Pakistan Plan to Check Petroleum Smuggling: Pakistan Official." *BBC News*, December 13, 2002.

Jalalzai, Musa Khan. *The Sunni-Shi'a Conflict in Pakistan.* Lahore: Shirkat, 2002.

Jamal, Arif. *News on Sunday,* November 10, 2002.

Jamat-ud-Dawa. http://www.jamatuddawa.org/English2/index.htm (accessed December 30, 2005).

Kapisthalam, Kaushik. "Outside View: Pakistani Jihadis in Iraq." *Washington Times Online*, July 5, 2004. http://washingtontimes.com/upi-breaking/20040705-123700-2711r.htm (accessed September 23, 2005).

"Karachi Bomb 'Terrorist Murders.'" CNN.com, May 09, 2002. http:// archives.cnn.com/2002/WORLD/asiapcf/south/05/08/pakistan. bombing/?related (accessed June 27, 2005).

Kennedy, Charles. "Islamicization and Legal Reform in Pakistan, 1979-1989." *Pacific Affairs*, no. 63 (spring 1990).

Khan, Azmat Hayat. "FATA." In *Tribal Areas of Pakistan: Challenges and Responses*, edited by Pervaiz Iqbal Cheema and Maqsudul Hasan Nuri. Islamabad: Islamabad Policy Institute, 2005.

Khan, Foqia Sadiq and Shahrukh Rafi Khan. *A Benchmark Study on Law-And-Order and the Dispensation of Justice in the Context of Power Devolution.* Islamabad: SDPI: 2003.

Khan, Farooq. "Black Business: Smuggling Picks Up Under the ATTA." *Daily Times* (Pakistan), November 18, 2004.

Khan, Kamran and Susan Schmidt. "Key 9/11 Suspect Leaves Pakistan in U.S. Custody." *Washington Post*, September 17, 2002.

Khan, M. Ilyas. "Ready to Rumple." *Herald* (Pakistan), August 2004.

———. "Who Are These People." *Herald* (Pakistan), April 2004.

———. "The Waiting Game." *Herald* (Pakistan), July 2003.

———. "Business as Usual." *Herald* (Pakistan), July 2003.

Khan, Rashid Ahmad Khan. "Political Developments in FATA: A Critical Perspective." In *Tribal Areas of Pakistan,* edited by Pervaiz Iqbal Cheema and Maqsudul Hasan Nuri, 25–42. Islamabad, Islamabad Policy Research Institute, 2005.

Khattak, Saba Gul, Shafi ur Rehman, and Saeed Shafgat. *Perspectives on Corruption in Pakistan: A Pilot Study.* Islamabad: Sustainable Development Policy Institute, 1999.

"Killing of Sunni Cleric Spurs Riots in Pakistan." *Los Angeles Times*, May 31, 2004.

Kronstadt, K. Alan. *International Terrorism in South Asia*, Congressional Research Service Report RS21658. Washington, D.C.: Congressional Research Service, November 3, 2003.

———. *Pakistan-U.S. Relations.* Congressional Research Service Report IB94041. Washington, D.C.: Congressional Research Service, July 26, 2006. http://www.fas.org/sgp/crs/row/IB94041.pdf (accessed October 6, 2005).

Kronstadt, K. Alan and Bruce Vaughn. *Terrorism in South Asia.* Washington, D.C.: Congressional Research Service, August 9, 2004.

Lancaster, John and Kamran Khan. "Investigation of Attacks on Musharraf Points to Pakistani Group." *Washington Post*, January 14, 2004.

"Lashkar-e-Jhangvi." MIPT Terrorism Knowledgebase. http://tkb.org/Group.jsp?groupID=65 (accessed October 3, 2005).

Lichtarowicz, Ania. "Aids Fear in Pakistan." *BBC News Online*, July 10, 2003. http://news.bbc.co.uk/go/pr/fr/-/2/hi/south_asia/3055009.stm (accessed October 11, 2003).

Lieven, Anatol. "The Pressures on Pakistan." *Foreign Affairs* 81, no. 1 (2002).

Loof, Susanna. "U.N. Agency Warns Afghanistan Over Opium." *Guardian* (UK), October 29, 2003.

Looney, Robert. "Strategic Insight—A U.S. Strategy for Achieving Stability in Pakistan: Expanding Educational Opportunities." September 2, 2002. http://www.ccc.nps.navy.mil/rsepResources/si/sept02/southAsia.asp.

Malik, Nadeem. "15 to 20 pc Madaris Impart Military Training: WB." *News International* (Pakistan), August 2, 2002.

Marawat, Akhatar. Interview by author. Ministry of Interior, Islamabad, Pakistan, January 2005.

Masood, Salmon. "Musharraf Vows Crackdown." *National Post* (Canada), December 26, 2003.

———. "Pakistan Bans Public Meetings After 40 Die in a Car Bombing." *New York Times*, October 8, 2004.

———. "Suicide Bomber Kills 3 Others at a Shiite Mosque in Pakistan." *New York Times*, October 11, 2004.

McDougall, Dan. "Government's Earthquake Aid Failure Fuels Calls for Holy War." *Scotsman*, October 16, 2005. http://www.jamatuddawa.org/English2/news/200510/19/failure.htm (accessed December 30, 2005).

McGirk, Tim and Hanna Bloch, "Has Pakistan Tamed its Spies?" *Time*, May 6, 2003.

"Military Operations in FATA." PakDef.Info.com. http://www.pakdef.info/forum/showthread.php?t=5599 (accessed September 23, 2005).

Ministry of Foreign Affairs. Interview by author. Islamabad, January 2005.

Mir, Amir. *True Face of the Jehadis*. Lahore: Mashall, 2004.

Musharraf, Pervez. "From the President's Desk." http://www.presidentofpakistan.gov.pk/FromThePresidentsDesk.aspx (accessed January 5, 2006).

————. "A Plea for Enlightened Moderation: Muslims Must Raise Themselves Up through Individual Achievement and Socioeconomic Emancipation." *Washington Post*, June 1, 2004.

"Masharraf's New Pakistan: What the People Think." *Herald* (Pakistan), February 2002.

"Musharraf's Move." *Economist*, January 12, 2002.

Mustafa, Zubeida. "A Curriculum of Hatred." *Link*, April 4, 2004. http:// www.pakistanlink.com/Letters/2004/April04/09/02.html (accessed September 10, 2005).

Nadeem, Azhar Hassan. *Pakistan: The Political Economy of Lawlessness*. Karachi: Oxford University Press, 2002.

Nasr, Seyyed Vali Reza. "International Politics, Domestic Imperatives and Identity Mobilization: Sectarianism in Pakistan, 1979–1988." *Comparative Politics* 2, no. 2 (2000).

National Anti-Corruption Strategy Report—2002. Islamabad: National Accountability Bureau, 2002.

National Integrity Systems. *Transparency International Country Study Report—Pakistan 2003*. Berlin: Transparency International, 2003.

Niaz, Colonel G.H. "Stop the Spread of Drug Addiction in Pakistan." *Pakistan News Service*, June 27, 2004. http://paknews.com/art1 jun-27.html.

Nuri, Maqsudul Hassan. *Tribal Areas of Pakistan: Challenges and Responses*. Islamabad: Islamabad Policy Institute, 2005.

Obaid, Sharmeen. "Pakistan: The Hunt for Osama Bin Laden." *Frontline World*, September 14, 2004. http://www.pbs.org/frontlineworld/ elections/pakistan/ (accessed October 2, 2005).

Office of Antiterrorism Assistance. http://www.diplomaticsecurity.org/ (accessed July 7, 2005).

"Oh, What a Lovely Ally." *Economist*, October 19, 2002.

"Pak Admits Dawood's Presence in Karachi." News, September 21, 2003. http://www.jang.com.pk/thenews/sep2003-daily/21-09-2003/ main/update.shtml.

"Pak on High Alert as Militant Reveals Plot to Attack Shiites." Associated Press, July 02, 2004.

Pakistan ANF. Interview by author. Islamabad, Pakistan, January 2005.

"Pakistan Asked to Explain Islamic Party Link to Al Qaeda Suspects." Agence France-Presse, March 3, 2003.

"Pakistan Border Unit Gets Boost From U.S." *Washington Post*, December 18, 2002.

"Pakistan Gears Up To Tackle People Smugglers." Agence France-Presse, February 20, 2003.

Pakistan Development Policy Review. New York: World Bank, 2002.

"Pakistan: Entire Election Deeply Flawed." Human Rights Watch Background Briefing. New York: Human Rights Watch, October 9, 2002.

"Pakistan Extends Qaeda Deadline." CBS News Online, April 19, 2004. http://www.cbsnews.com/stories/2004/04/21/terror/main 612988.shtml (accessed September 10, 2005).

Pakistan Federal Investigative Agency officials. Interview by author. Islamabad, Pakistan, January 2005.

"Pakistan Funds Islamic Terror." *Sunday Telegraph* (UK), May 16, 1999.

"Pakistan: IOM Launches Counter Trafficking Course." UN Office for the Coordination of Humanitarian Affairs, July 27, 2004. http://www.irinnews.org/report.asp?ReportID=42384&SelectRegion=Central_Asia&SelectCountry=PAKISTAN (accessed August 30, 2005).

"Pakistan Launches Terror Raid." CBS News Online, March 16, 2004. http://www.cbsnews.com/stories/2004/03/18/terror/main 607118.shtml (accessed October 3, 2005).

"Pakistan—Newly Established Anti-Trafficking Unit Receives IOM Training." IOM Press, May 17, 2005.

"Pak Shuts Down ISI Cell in Afghanistan." *Tribune* (Chandigarh), February 20, 2002. http://www.tribuneindia.com/2002/20020221/world .htm#8 (accessed October 10, 2005).

"Pakistan MPs Protest Over Arrest." *BBC News Online*, October 31, 2003. http://news.bbc.co.uk/2/hi/south_asia/3230879.stm (accessed December 28, 2005).

"Pakistani Mosque Bombed; 16 Killed." *Los Angeles Times*, June 1, 2004.

Pakistan's Anti-Corruption Program: Observations and Recommendations. Berlin: Transparency International, 2002.

"Pakistan's Fight Against Corruption: Problems and Prospects." Speech delivered by the chairman of the National Accountability Bureau at the International Institute for Strategic Studies, March 16, 2005. http://www.iiss.org/showdocument.php?docID=647 (accessed January 5, 2006).

"Pakistan's Wild Frontier." *Al Jazeera Net*, March 20, 2004. http://english. aljazeera.net/NR/exeres/8BE012FB-EE25-4424-8153-23CE43 BE3152.htm (accessed October 2, 2005).

Patel, Y.I. "Dig Vijay to Divya Astra—A Paradigm Shift in the Indian Army's Doctrine." *Bharat Rakshak Monitor* 6, no. 6 (2004). http:// www.bharat-rakshak.com/MONITOR/ISSUE6-6/patel.html (accessed October 3, 2005).

"Petroleum Products Smuggling Rampant in Pakistan." *Pakistan Newswire*, April 11, 2003.

Pew Research Center. "U.S. Image Up Slightly, But Still Negative American Character Gets Mixed Reviews." Pew Research Center, June 2005. http://pewglobal.org/reports/display.php?ReportID=247 (accessed September 10, 2005).

Piracha, Shaukat. "3 more Religious Outfits Banned." *Daily Times*, November 21, 2003. http://www.dailytimes.com.pk/default.asp?page= story_21-11-2003_pg1_3 (accessed October 10, 2005).

Police Order, 2002 Chief Executive's Order No. 22 of 2002. August 14, 2002. Lahore: Manzoor Law Book House, 2005.

Powell, Nancy J. "U.S. Foreign Policy Towards Pakistan." August 20, 2004. http://www.state.gov/p/sa/rls/rm/35681.htm (accessed September 28, 2005).

———. "U.S. Foreign Policy Towards Pakistan," November 13, 2003. http://www.state.gov/p/sa/rls/rm/26277.htm (accessed July 14, 2005).

"PTA For Cut in Import Duty on Tea." *Pakistan Newswire*, May 14, 2003.

Rabasa, Angel, ed. *The Muslim World and the United States After 9/11 and the Iraq War*. Santa Monica, Calif.: RAND, 2004.

Raman, B. "Murder and Machination in Pakistan's Backyard." *Asia Times*, July 10, 2003.

Rana, Muhammad Amir. *The A to Z of Jehadi Organizations in Pakistan*. Lahore: Mashal, 2004.

Rashid, Ahmed. "Pakistan Army Officers Arrested in Terror Swoop." *Daily Telegraph* (UK), September 1, 2003

———. "Islamists Impose Taliban-Type Morals Monitors." *Daily Telegraph* (UK), June 3, 2003.

———. "Musharraf's Bin Laden Headache." *BBC News Online*. http://news.bbc.co.uk/2/hi/south_asia/3545985.stm (accessed October 3, 2005).

———. *Taliban: Islam, Oil and the New Great Game in Central Asia*. London: I.B Tauris, 2001.

Raza, Shahzad. "Rising HIV/AIDS Cases in Pakistan: Prime Minister to Chair HIV/AIDS Meeting Today." *Daily Times* (Pakistan), November 8, 2004.

Rahman, Tariq. "Pluralism and Intolerance in Pakistani Society Attitudes of Pakistani Students Towards the Religious 'Other.'" Presented at conference on pluralism at the Agha Khan University-Institute for the Study of Muslim Civilization, October 25, 2003. http://www.aku.edu/news/majorevents/ismcconf-tr.pdf (accessed October 3, 2005).

Risen, James and David Rohde. "Mountains and Border Foil Quest for Bin Laden." *New York Times*, December 13, 2004.

Rizvi, Hasan-Askari. "A Moderate and Enlightened Pakistan." *Daily Times* (Pakistan), January 17, 2005.

Robson, Brian. *Crisis on the Frontier: The Third Afghan War and the Campaign in Waziristan 1919–1920.* London: Spellmount Publishers, 2004.

Rocca, Christina. United States Interests and Foreign Policy Priorities in South Asia. Testimony prepared for the U.S. House of Representatives Committee on International Relations, given June 22, 2004. http://wwwc.house.gov/international_relations/108/roc062204.htm (accessed August 30, 2005).

Rohde, David. "Two Years Later: Islamic Ally: Questions Grow on Pakistan's Commitment to Fight Taliban." *New York Times,* September 10, 2003.

Rohde, David, et al. "Pakistan Battle Pierces Solitude Of Tribal Area." *New York Times,* March 21, 2004.

Rowen, Henry, ed. *Prospects for Peace in South Asia.* Palo Alto, Calif.: Stanford University Press, 2005.

Saeed, Abrar. "Top al-Qaeda Operative Arrested in Pindi." *Nation,* March 2, 2003.

Sayyed, Tashbih. "Exclusive Interview: Justice (R) Sajjad Ali Shah." *Pakistan Today,* October 15, 1999. http://www.paktoday.com/shah.htm (accessed January 5, 2006).

Scarborough, Rowan. "Osama bin Laden a 'Narco-Terrorist.'" *Washington Times,* January 22, 2004.

Schaffer, Terasita. *Pakistan's Future and U.S. Policy Options.* Washington, D.C.: CSIS, March 2004.

Schmitt, Eric. "Afghan's Gains Threatened by Drug Traffic." *New York Times,* December 11, 2004.

Sciolino, Elaine and D. Van Natta. "2004 British Raid Sounded Alert on Pakistani Militants." *New York Times,* July 14, 2005.

———. "Searching for Footprints." *New York Times,* July 25, 2005.

Shad, Ashraf. "Dawood Ibrahim Not Seen at Daughter's Wedding: Grand Show at Dubai Hotel." *Dawn,* July 25, 2005. http://dawn.com/2005/07/25/top13.htm (accessed August 8, 2005).

Shah, Marshuk Ali. "Asian Development Bank's Anti-Corruption Initiatives." Conference on Combating Corruption in the Public and Private Sector, Islamabad, August 20, 2004.

Sharp, Jeremy M. *Egypt-United States Relations.* Congressional Research Service Report IB93087. Washington, D.C.: Congressional Research Service, June 15, 2005. http://www.fas.org/sgp/crs/mideast/IB93087.p (accessed October 10, 2005).

Sharma, Rajeev. "Pakistan's Talibanisation." In *The Pakistan Trap*, edited by Rajeev Sharma. New Delhi: UBS Publishers, 2001.

Shahzad, Syed Saleem. "Pakistan-India: Same Game, New Rule." *Asia Times*, November 27, 2003. http://www.atimes.com/atimes/South_Asia/EK27Df03.html (accessed October 10, 2005).

Shaw, Mark. "West African Criminal Networks in South and Southern Africa."*African Affairs* 101 (2002).

Shigri, Afzal A. "Institutionalizing Political Interference in Policing." *News*, December 8, 2004.

———. "Policing the Police." *News*, April 10, 2004.

Simons, Paul. *Starving Terrorists of Money: The Role of the Middle East Financial Institutions.* Prepared for the House Committee on International Relations, Subcommittee on International Terrorism and Non-proliferation and House Financial Services Subcommittee on Oversight and Investigations, May 4, 2005. http://wwwc.house.gov/international_relations/109/sim050405.pdf. (accessed July 14, 2005).

Singer, Peter W. "Pakistan's Madrassahs: Ensuring a System of Education not Jihad." Analysis Papers 41. Washington, D.C.: Brookings Institution, 2001.

"Sipah-e-Mohammed Pakistan, Terrorist Group of Pakistan." *South Asia Terrorism Portal.* http://www.satp.org/satporgtp/countries/pakistan/terroristoutfits/SMP.htm (accessed August 29 2005).

"Smuggling on Rise on GT Road, Motorway." *Pakistan Press International*, October 23, 2003.

"South Africa Becomes Major Hub in Global Drug Trafficking." *Janes Intelligence Review*, July 2005.

Spillers, Alex and Philip Broughton. "Al-Qa'eda Suicide Bomb Kills 14." *Daily Telegraph* (UK), June 27, 2005.

Stern, Jessica. "Pakistan's Jihad Culture." *Foreign Affairs* 79, no. 6 (2000).

Strathdee, Steffanie. "The Rise in Needle Sharing Among Drug Users in Pakistan During the Afghanistan War." *Journal of Drug and Alcohol Dependence* (July 2003).

"'Suicide Attack' Hits Karachi Mosque." *BBC News Online*, May 7, 2004. http://newsvote.bbc.co.uk/.

"Suicide Squad to Battle Western Forces: LeT." *Times of India*, June 13, 2004.

Swami, Praveen. "Riding the Jehadi Tiger." *Herald*, Vol. 3, no. 11, May 2004. http://www.kashmirherald.com/featuredarticle/jehaditiger.html (accessed September 23, 2005).

Talbot, Ian. "General Pervez Musharraf: Savior or Destroyers of Pakistan's Democracy?" *Contemporary Southeast Asia* 11, no. 3, 2002.

Tandy, Karen. *Afghanistan: Law Enforcement Interdiction Efforts in Transshipment Countries to Stem the Flow of Heroin*. Report prepared for the U.S. House of Representatives Subcommittee on Criminal Justice, Drug Policy and Human Resources Committee on Government Reform, February 26, 2004. http://www.usdoj.gov/dea/pubs/cngrtest/ct022604.htm (accessed July 10, 2005).

Tellis, Ashley J. "U.S. Strategy: Assisting Pakistan's Transformation." *Washington Quarterly* 28, no. 1 (Winter 2004–2005).

Tellis, Ashley J., C. Christine Fair, and Jamison Jo Medby. *Limited Conflicts Under the Nuclear Umbrella—Indian and Pakistani Lessons from the Kargil Crisis*. Santa Monica, Calif.: RAND, 2001.

Terzieff, Juliette. "Assassination Tries Linked to al-Qaeda." *San Francisco Chronicle*, January 16, 2004.

"Text of Draft Police Ordinance 2002." *News*, March 20–April 2, 2002.

The National Commission on Terrorist Attacks Upon the United States, the 9/11 Commission Report. New York: W.W. Norton, 2004.

"The Wild Frontier." *Economist*, April 12, 2003.

Transparency International—Kazakhstan. "Nine Out of Ten Developing Countries Urgently Need Practical Support to Fight Corruption, Highlights New Index." http://www.transparencykazakhstan.org/english/cpi2003.htm.

Transparency International—Pakistan. "About TI-Pakistan." http://www.transparency.org.pk/org/abouttipak.htm (accessed July 14, 2005).

"Two Elections: New Hopes and Old Frustrations." *South Asia Monitor*, November 1, 2002.

Ulph, Stephen. "Jihadists Respond to Earthquake Victims in Pakistan." *Terrorism Focus* 2, no. 20 (2005).

"UN-Drugs-Pakistan: Risk of HIV Rises in Pakistan's Half Million Heroin Addicts." Agence France-Presse, February 26, 2003.

United Nations Office of Drugs and Crime. *The Opium Economy in Afghanistan: An International Problem.* New York: United Nations, 2003.

U.S. Agency for International Development. "Budget Justification to the Congress: Fiscal Year 2006." http://www.usaid.gov/policy/budget/cbj2006/ane/pk.html (accessed July 14, 2005).

———. "Pakistan Data Sheet: Democracy and Governance, FY 2004." http://www.usaid.gov/our_work/democracy_and_governance/regions/ane/pakistan.pdf (accessed July 14, 2005).

———. "USAID Pakistan Program Data Sheet 391-004." http://www.usaid.gov/pubs/cbj2003/ane/pk/391-004.html (accessed August 22, 2005).

U.S. Agency for International Development—Pakistan. "Democracy and Governance: Background." http://www.usaid.gov/pk/governance/ (accessed July 14, 2005).

———. "FATA School Rehabilitation and Refurbishment." April 8, 2005. http://www.usaid.gov/pk/program_sectors/education/projects/fata_school_rehabilitation.shtml (accessed July 8, 2005).

———. "USAID Pakistan Interim Strategic Plan: May 2003-September 2006." May 2003. http://www.usaid.gov/pk/isp/Interim_Strategic_Plan_03_06.shtml (accessed July 7, 2005).

U.S. Bureau for International Narcotics and Law Enforcement Affairs. "Bilateral Activities." *International Narcotics Control Strategy Report, 2005.* http://www.state.gov/g/inl/rls/nrcrpt/2005/vol2/html/42384.htm (accessed September 15, 2005).

———. "International Narcotics and Law Enforcement: FY 2004 Budget Justification." http://www.state.gov/p/inl/rls/rpt/cbj/fy2004/21884.htm (accessed September 28, 2005).

———. "Southwest Asia." *International Narcotics Control Strategy Report, 2002.* Washington, D.C.: United States Department of State, March 2003.

———. "Southwest Asia." *International Narcotics Control Strategy Report, 2003.* Washington, D.C.: United States Department of State, March 2004.

———. "Southwest Asia." *International Narcotics Control Strategy Report, 2004.* Washington, D.C.: United States Department of State, March 2005.

———. "U.S. Government Assistance." *International Narcotics Control Strategy Report, 2005.* http://www.state.gov/g/inl/rls/nrcrpt/2005/vol1/html/42361.htm (accessed July 7, 2005).

U.S. Central Command. Statement of General John P. Abizaid, United States Army Commander, United States Central Command before the House Armed Services Committee on the 2005 Posture of the United States Central Command, March 2, 2005. http://www.defense.gov/dodgc/olc/docs/test05-03-02Abizaid.doc (accessed October 6, 2005).

U.S. Department of Justice. "ICITAP Project Overviews for Pakistan." http://www.usdoj.gov/criminal/icitap/TextPakistan.html (accessed August 30, 2005).

U.S. Department of State. *Victims of Trafficking and Violence Protection Act of 2000: Trafficking in Persons Report, 2004.* http://www.state.gov/g/tip/rls/tiprpt/2004/.

———. *Victims of Trafficking and Violence Protection Act of 2000: Trafficking in Persons Report, 2005.* http://www.state.gov/g/tip/rls/tiprpt/2005/ (accessed August 9, 2005).

————. "Joint Statement of the Meeting of the Pakistan-U.S. Joint Working Group on Counter-Terrorism and Law Enforcement," September 3, 2004. http://www.state.gov/p/sa/rls/pr/35966.htm (accessed July 19, 2005).

————. "Media Note: Office of the Spokesman—Second Annual U.S.-Pakistan Joint Working Group on Counterterrorism and Law Enforcement," April 15, 2003. http://www.state.gov/r/pa/prs/ps/2003/19666.htm (accessed January 26, 2004).

————. *An Overview of INL Programs in Pakistan: Combating Terrorism, Narcotics Production, and Trafficking.* Prepared by INL official, November 29, 2004.

————. "U.S.-Pakistan Joint Group on Counter-Terrorism Meets." International Information Programs, May 8, 2002. http://usinfo.state.gov/regiona/nea/sasia/text/0508uspak.htm.

U.S. Department of State, Bureau of Democracy, Human Rights and Labor. *Pakistan Country Report on Human Rights Practices–2004*, February 28, 2005. http://www.state.gov/g/drl/rls/hrrpt/2004/41743.htm (accessed September 23, 2005).

U.S. Department of State. Bureau for International Narcotics and Law Enforcement Affairs. *International Narcotics Control Strategy Report.* Washington, D.C.: United States Department of State, March 2005.

U.S. Department of State, Career Transition Center. Interview by author. Washington, D.C., November 2004.

U.S. Department of State Official. Interview by author. Washington, D.C., November 2004.

U.S. Department of State, South Asia Regional Affairs Officials. Interviews by author. Washington, D.C., November 2004.

U.S. Department of Treasury. "U.S.-Based Branch of Al Haramain Foundation Linked to Terror: Treasury Designates U.S. Branch." JS-1895, September 8, 2004. http://www.ustreas.gov/press/releases/js1895.htm (accessed September 2, 2005).

U.S. Embassy, Islamabad. "USAID Provides $147 Million to Improve Pakistan's Health, Education, Economic, Governance Sectors," May

26, 2005. http://www.state.gov/p/sa/rls/pr/2005/46815.htm
(accessed July 7, 2005).

U.S. Office of the Coordinator for Counterterrorism. *Patterns of Global
Terrorism 2002*. Washington, D.C.: United States Department of
State, 2003.

U.S. Treasury. "U.S.-Based Branch of Al Haramain Foundation Linked to
Terror: Treasury Designates U.S. Branch." JS-1895, September 8,
2004. http://www.ustreas.gov/press/releases/js1895.htm (accessed
September 2, 2005).

Varshney, Ashutosh. "India, Pakistan and Kashmir: Antinomies of Nationalism." *Asian Survey* (November 1991).

Waldman, Amy. "Pakistan Arrests Militant With Ties to Taliban." *New
York Times*, August 9, 2004.

Walsh, Declan. "Pakistani Extremists Take Lead on Earthquake Disaster
Aid: International Relief Agencies Are Only Beginning to Arrive."
San Francisco Chronicle, October 17, 2005.

Warren, Alan. *Waziristan, the Faqir of Ipi, and the Indian Army: The North
West Frontier Revolt of 1936–37*. Oxford: Oxford University Press,
1999.

Waslekar, Sundeep, Leena Pillai, and Shabnam Siddiqui. *The Future of
Pakistan*. Mumbai: International Centre for Peace Initiatives, 2002.

Watson, Paul and Mubashir Zaidi. "Militant Flourishes in Plain Sight."
Los Angeles Times, January 25, 2004.

Wayne, Anthony. *International Dimension of Combating the Financing of
Terrorism*. Prepared for the House Committee on International Relations, Subcommittee on International Terrorism, Nonproliferation
and Human Rights, March 26, 2003. http://www.state.gov/e/eb/
rls/rm/2003/19113.htm (accessed July 10, 2005).

Wirsing, Robert. *India, Pakistan and the Kashmir Dispute*. London: Macmillan, 1994.

World Bank. "Pakistan's Reform Program: Progress and Prospects Report."
http://wbln1018.worldbank.org/sar/sa.nsf/083c4661ad49652
f852567d7005d85b8/c3e79a8d2720625385256a090074d943?
OpenDocument (accessed February 3, 2003).

Wylly, H. C. *Tribes of Central Asia, from the Black Mountain to Waziristan*. Lahore: Vanguard Books, 1996.

Yasin, Mohammad and Tariq Banuri. *The Dispensation of Justice in Pakistan*. Islamabad: Oxford, 2004.

Yusufzai, Rahimullah. "Waziristan: Bin Laden's hiding place?" *BBC News Online*, March 4, 2004. http://news.bbc.co.uk/1/hi/world/south_asia/3532841.stm (accessed October 3, 2005).

Zaidi, S. Hussain. *Black Friday: The True Story of the Bombay Bomb Blasts*. New Delhi: Penguin Books India, 2003.

Zaman, Muhammad Qasim. "Sectarianism in Pakistan: The Radicalization of Shi'a and Sunni Identities." *Modern Asian Studies* 32, no. 3 (1998).

Index

A

Afghan Transit Trade Agreement
  goods smuggling and, 34
Afghanistan
  Afghan opium statistics, 1994–2003 (table), 30
  opium production, 28
  reversal of U.S. policy toward, 1
  salaam loan system, 100 *n*108
AFIS. See Automated Fingerprint Identification System
Ajmal, Muhammad
  Lashkar-e-Jhangvi founding and, 26
ANF. *See* Anti-Narcotics Task Force
Anti-Narcotics Task Force
  Drug Enforcement Agency efforts and, 52, 56
  funding concerns, 75–76, 118 *n*47
  HIV/AIDS crisis and, 76
Armed forces
  corruption and, 41–42
  earthquake response, 81
Armitage, Richard
  Musharraf's pledge to end cross-border infiltration of terrorists into
        Jammu and Kashmir and, 16, 91 *n*32
Assessment of U.S. assistance programs
  balancing security concerns with open and responsible government,
        78–79
  civil society and, 70–71, 117 *n*35
  compensatory, organizational, and geographic problems, 67
  geographic concentration of counterterrorism assistance, 72
  hard security bias, 72
  institutional challenges within domestic police and intelligence agencies,
        65–67
  language barrier and, 73, 118 *n*43
  lease arrangements for equipment and, 73–74
  legislative frameworks and, 69–70
  limitations to the success of, 61
  nuclear capabilities and, 4–5, 71, 78–79, 117 *n*31

---

n preceding a number indicates a note.

overview of threats and U.S. assistance programs, 61–64

Pakistan's willingness and/or ability to crack down on Islamist militants, 67–69, 74–75

problems associated with the U.S. provision of security assistance, 70–74

programmatic implementation and assessment, 72–73

recommendations, 74–77

shortcomings specific to Pakistan's contribution to the bilateral security engagement, 64–70

statutory problems, 66

structural impediments to effective implementation, 73–74

U.S. security assistance and the extant Pakistani internal threat environment (table), 63

ATTA. *See* Afghan Transit Trade Agreement

Automated Fingerprint Identification System

development of, 51, 55, 112 *n*58

usefulness of, 61

Azhar, Masood

Jaish-e-Mohammad role, 16

Aziz, Prime Minister Shaukat

assassination attempts against, 17, 48

B

al Badr

composition of, 15

Pakistani intelligence control of, 17

Baluchistan

drug traffic route through, 29

INL view of, 47

"police operations" in, 87 *n*1

poppy eradication efforts in, 56

Basra, Riaz

Lashkar-e-Jhangvi founding and, 26

Bhutto, Benazir

Pakistan's People Party leader, 70

Bin Laden, Osama

assassination attempts against Musharraf and, 14

Binalshib, Ramzi

capture of, 15

Bribes. *See* Corruption

Bureau of Diplomatic Security, Office of Antiterrorism Assistance. *See* Counterterrorism Office and Bureau of Diplomatic Security, Office of Antiterrorism Assistance

Bureau of International Narcotics and Law Enforcement
  aims of programs in Pakistan, 47
  Border Security Project, 52, 54
  counternarcotics programming, 56
  expansion of ground mobility capabilities, 53
  Forward Operating Base project, 53, 111 *n*41
  Frontier Corps training and, 53
  funding to help fortify border areas, 47
  ICITAP and, 50, 54, 109 *n*26
  Narcotics Coordination Cells, 56
  Personal Identification Security, Comparison and Evaluation System and,
      52
  police training programs, 54
  road-building projects, 53, 56
  terrain issues, 47
  travel security issues, 73, 118 *n*41

C

Children. *See* Goods smuggling and human trafficking
China
  training facilities and equipment for the creation of a DNA lab, 56
Coalition Support Funds
  payments received by Pakistan, 86 *n*24
Corruption
  armed forces and, 41–42
  average bribe per sector (table), 39
  commercial enterprises and, 42–43
  criminal justice system and, 43
  development projects and, 42
  drug trafficking and, 33
  estimates of payouts, 38–39
  feudal family structure and, 39–40
  goods smuggling and human trafficking and, 36
  government involvement in commercial activity and, 40–41
  impact on stability, 42–43
  judiciary and, 3, 40, 43, 106 *n*164
  limitations of assistance and, 66–67
  literacy rates and, 42, 107 *n*178
  loss of public revenue and, 42
  most corrupt sectors in Pakistan according to public opinion (table), 38
  politicized bureaucracy and, 40
  recommendations for programming, 76–77

roots and causes of, 39–40

success in addressing the threat from, 62–64

Transparency International's Corruption Perception Index, 37–38, 40, 105 *n*154

World Bank definition, 105 *n*153

Corruption Perception Index

scores for Pakistan, 2–3, 37–38, 40, 85 *n*10, 105 *n*154

Counterterrorism Office and Bureau of Diplomatic Security, Office of Antiterrorism Assistance

border security class, 53–54

criteria for assistance from, 49

development of investigative skills in the civilian sector and, 48

efforts by Pakistan to thwart terrorism and, 48–49

S/CT goals and budget for Pakistan, 48

training and development goals, 49–50

CPI. *See* Corruption Perception Index

CSF. *See* Coalition Support Funds

D

DEA. *See* Drug Enforcement Agency

Democracy and Good Governance program

focus of, 57–58

Deobandi

proscription of, 90 *n*27

reorientation of Kashmir-focused groups, 15–18, 22

roots and tradition of, 90 *n*26

Domestic threat environment

corruption, 37–43, 62–64

drugs trafficking, 28–33, 62, 75–76

goods smuggling and human trafficking, 33–37, 62

jihadist terrorism, 1–2, 9–24, 61–62, 77

overview, 7, 61–64

sectarian violence, 1–2, 24–28, 62, 77, 96 *n*79

Drug Enforcement Agency

Anti-Narcotics Task Force and, 52, 56

heroin containment strategy, 52, 110 *n*36

Special Investigative Units in Pakistan, 52, 56

Drugs trafficking. *See also* Bureau of International Narcotics and Law Enforcement; Drug Enforcement Agency

Afghan opium statistics, 1994–2003 (table), 30

border security and, 29, 31, 100 *n*110

capacity to treat drug users, 31

corruption and, 33

costs associated with the control of opium imports, 33

destination points, 29

drug-related crime, 32–33

factors in the increase of, 28

HIV/AIDS and, 32

increase in drug production in Afghanistan, 28–29

needle sharing study, 102 *n*124

opiate seizures and drug arrests in Pakistan, 1996–2004 (table), 30

ports on the Makran coast and, 29, 101 *n*112

primary drug transit route, 29

public health issues, 31

recommendations for programming, 75–76

"scatter-gun" approach to smuggling, 29

secondary markets, 29

street value of heroin, 29, 101 *n*116

success in addressing the threat from, 62

weak legal and regulatory financial systems and, 31, 101 *n*120

DS/ATA. *See* Counterterrorism Office and Bureau of Diplomatic Security, Office of Antiterrorism Assistance

E

Earthquake of 2005

army's response to, 81

estimate of the number killed, 81

international relief assistance, 119 *n*1

militant groups' response to, 81–82

Educational institutions

enrollment estimates for *madaris*, 19

government policy toward *madaris*, 20

madrassah reform program, 20, 23, 67–68, 115 *n*17

public school curriculum reform, 20–21

radicalizing influences of *madaris*, 18–21

terrorist training and, 19

Enlightened moderation

criticism of, 68–69, 115 *n*22

description, 91 *n*36

expansion of radical Islamist sentiment and, 22–23

Musharraf's call for, 17

F

Farooqui, Amjad Hussain
  assassination attempts against Musharraf and Hayat and, 22
  work with Shaikh and al-Libbi, 22
FATA. *See* Federally Administered Tribal Areas
FATF. *See* Financial Action Task Force
FC. *See* Frontier Constabulary; Frontier Corps
FCR. *See* Frontier Crime Regulation
Federal Investigative Agency
  human trafficking estimate, 34
  Special Investigative Groups, 69
Federally Administered Tribal Areas
  administrative political agencies, 87 *n*3
  agency administrative structure (figure), 11
  collective responsibility tenet and, 12
  colonial-era system and, 10
  foreign jihadist activities in, 9–15
  Frontier Crime Regulation, 12
  governing arrangements, 10–12
  INL view of, 47
  maliks and, 10–12
  map, xx
  melmastia and, 12–13
  military operations against suspected terrorists seeking refuge in, 87 *n*6
  mullah-*malik* relationship, 13
  Northwest Frontier Province governor's responsibilities, 10
  Pakhtun majority in, 12, 88 *n*13
  pakhtunwali and, 12–13
  political agents' responsibilities, 10–12
  recommendations for programming, 77
  relocation of militants from Afghanistan to, 9–10
  Soviet invasion of Afghanistan and, 12–13
  support for al-Qaeda and the Taliban, 67
  urban districts and, 15
  Wahabbists and, 13
FIA. *See* Federal Investigative Agency
Financial Action Task Force
  terrorism programs and, 113 *n*72
Financial Intelligence Units
  terrorism programs and, 57, 113 *n*72
FIUs. *See* Financial Intelligence Units

Forensic laboratories, 3, 51, 54, 85 *n*11, 111 *n*54, 111 *n*55
Former Soviet Union
invasion of Afghanistan, 12–13
Forward Operating Base project
description, 53
geographic restrictions on, 72, 117 *n*39
usefulness of, 61
Frontier Constabulary
FATA responsibilities, 11
Frontier Corps
Bureau of International Narcotics and Law Enforcement training, 53
FATA responsibilities, 11
support for drugs trafficking measures, 76, 119 *n*49
Frontier Crime Regulation
collective responsibility tenet, 12

G

Ghailani, Ahmed
al-Qaeda membership and, 84 *n*4
arrest of, 1
Global war on terror
jihadist terrorism and, 9, 14
Mutahida Majlis-e-Amal opposition to, 23
Pakistan as a central partner in, 1, 83 *n*3
S/CT goals and, 48
U.S. assistance to Pakistan and, 45, 58
Golden Crescent
countries included, 99 *n*102
Goods smuggling and human trafficking
black-market bazaars, 33–34
border issues, 35
corruption and, 36
countertrafficking training course, 57
effect on the national tea industry, 36
factors in the increase in, 35
hawala and, 34, 57, 103 *n*138
impact on stability, 35–37
International Organization for Migration and, 56–57
legislation needed for combating, 57, 112 *n*69
recommendations for programming, 76–77
success in addressing the threat from, 62
Tier 2 Watch List status and, 34–35

Tier 3 Watch List status and, 35, 104 *n*142
U.S. funding for initiatives against, 56–57
victim assistance efforts, 36, 104 *n*151
Great Britain
narcotics smuggling and, 62, 119 *n*48
GWOT. *See* Global war on terror

H

Haider, Moinuddin
Joint Working Group on Counter Terrorism and Law Enforcement role,
45–46
Haqqani, Husain
public school curriculum and, 20
Harakat-ul-Jihad-e-Islami
anti-Pakistani state stance, 17
assassination attempts against Musharraf and, 17
composition of, 15
Harkat-ul-Mujahadeen
anti-Pakistani state stance, 17
composition of, 15
proscription of, 67
Harvard University's Kennedy School of Government
study of *madaris*, 19, 20
Hashimi, Javed
charges of treason against, 41
Hawala
crackdown on, 103 *n*138
freezing of al-Qaeda assets and, 57
goods smuggling and, 34
Hayat, Lt. Gen. Ahsan Saleem
assassination attempts against, 17, 21, 48
HIV/AIDS
Anti-Narcotics Task Force and, 76
IV drug users and, 32
Hizbol Mujahadeen
composition of, 15
Pakistani intelligence control of, 17
HM. *See* Hizbol Mujahadeen
HuJI. *See* Harakat-ul-Jihad-e-Islam
HuM. *See* Harkat-ul-Mujahadeen
Human trafficking. *See* Goods smuggling and human trafficking

I

Ibrahim, Dawood
    drug trafficking and, 32, 102 *n*129
ICG. *See* International Crisis Group
ICITAP. *See* International Criminal Investigative Training Assistance
       Program
India
    attack on the Indian Parliament, 16, 23
    lack of an extradition treaty with Pakistan, 4, 86 *n*18
    limited-war doctrine, 24, 96 *n*78
    massacre of military wives and children in Kashmir, 16
    military standoff with Pakistan, 1, 16
    Pakistan's peace process with, 16
INL. *See* Bureau of International Narcotics and Law Enforcement
Instructional courses
    choice of participants for, 65–66
    courses offered, 54, 111 *n*51, 111 *n*52, 111 *n*53
    language barrier and, 73, 118 *n*43
    postcourse deployments, 66
Inter-Services Intelligence
    backing of jihadists, 2, 84 *n*7
    estimate of the number of *madaris*, 18
International Criminal Investigative Training Assistance Program
    aim of initiatives, 51–52
    Automated Fingerprint Identification System and, 51, 55, 112 *n*58
    border security and, 51, 54
    core areas for assistance, 51
    forensic laboratories and, 3, 51, 54, 85 *n*11, 111 *n*54, 111 *n*55
    INL and, 50, 54, 109 *n*26
    institution building within the national police force and, 54, 111 *n*49
    instructional courses offered in the United States, 54, 65–66, 111 *n*51, 111
       *n*52, 111 *n*53
    law enforcement reform and training and, 51
    National Criminal Data Base and, 51, 55
    percentage of law enforcement officers capable of investigative activities,
       51, 110 *n*31
    problems specific to Pakistan and, 50–51
    Special Investigative Groups and, 69
International Crisis Group
    estimates of *madari* enrollment, 19
    report on corruption in the judiciary, 40

International Organization for Migration
   funding for initiatives against human trafficking, 56–57
IOM. *See* International Organization for Migration
Ishaque, Malik
   Lashkar-e-Jhangvi founding and, 26
ISI. *See* Inter-Services Intelligence
ITMD. *See* Ittehad-e-Tanzeem ul-Madaris-e-Deeni
Ittehad-e-Tanzeem ul-Madaris-e-Deeni
   madrassah reform program and, 20
   registration of *madaris* and, 20

J

Jabbar, Maulana Abdul
   Jaish-e-Mohammad role, 16
Jaish-e-Mohammad
   assassination attempts against Musharraf and, 17
   assault on the Indian Parliament, 16
   attack on French engineers in Karachi and, 68
   composition of, 15
   links to al-Qaeda, 68
   links to Sunni sectarian organizations, 62
   London Underground attacks and, 18
   madaris and, 19
   "moderated-jihad" strategy and, 16
   overlapping membership with Sipah-e-Sahaba-Pakistan, 68
   Pakistan's relationship with the United States and, 15–16
   proscription of, 67
   splintering of, 17
Jamaat Islam
   earthquake response, 81–82
   opposition to the Musharraf regime, 21
Jamaat-ul-Furqaan
   targeting of Pakistan's government, 16
Jammu
   extradition disputes, 1
   limitation of militant activities in, 16
   map, xxi
   Musharraf's pledge to end cross-border infiltration of terrorists into
      Jammu and Kashmir, 16, 91 *n*32
JeM. *See* Jaish-e-Mohammad
Jhangvi, Maulana Haq Nawaz
   SSP founding, 25

JI. *See* Jamaat Islam
Jihadist terrorism
    antiterrorist financing programs, 57, 113 *n*72
    educational institution influence, 18–21
    Financial Action Task Force and, 57, 113 *n*72
    Financial Intelligence Unit creation and, 57
    foreign jihadist activities in Federally Administered Tribal Areas, 9–15
    harboring of Pakhtun militants, 68
    impact on stability, 22–24, 61–62
    lack of evidence to prosecute cases against, 67, 114 *n*16
    recommendations for programming, 77
    reorientation of Deobandi Kashmir-focused groups, 15–18
    security force involvement, 21–22
    success in addressing the threat from, 61–62
Jirga
    FATA administration and, 11
Joint Working Group on Counter Terrorism and Law Enforcement
    importance of, 65
    meetings and agenda, 3–4, 45–46
Judiciary
    corruption and, 3, 40–41, 43, 106 *n*164
JWG-CTLE. *See* Joint Working Group on Counter Terrorism and Law
        Enforcement

K

Karachi
    attack on French engineers in, 22, 68
    foreign jihadists hiding in, 15
    pilot criminal investigation division, 86 *n*22
    port security efforts, 66–67
Karachi Stock Exchange
    money laundering and, 36
    performance of, 98 *n*101
Kashmir
    extradition disputes, 1
    limitation of militant activities in, 16
    map, xxi
    Musharraf's pledge to end cross-border infiltration of terrorists into
        Jammu and Kashmir, 16, 91n32
    reorientation of Deobandi organizations and, 15–18
Kennedy School of Government. *See* Harvard University's Kennedy School
        of Government

Khan, Ayub
    public school curriculum and, 20
Khasadars
    responsibilities in FATA, 11
Khomeini, Ayatollah, 25

L

Lahori, Akram
    Lashkar-e-Jhangvi founding and, 26
Lashkar-e-Jhangvi
    attack on French engineers in Karachi and, 68
    estimated militant base of, 26
    founding of, 26
    links to al-Qaeda, 68
    links to other Islamist entities, 62
    overlapping membership with Sipah-e-Sahaba Pakistan, 68
    reorientation of, 22
Lashkar-e-Taiba
    al-Qaeda and, 18
    anti-Western positions, 92 *n*39
    composition of, 15
    earthquake response, 81–82
    globalization and, 17
    links to Sunni sectarian organizations, 62
    London Underground attacks and, 18
    madaris and, 19
    massacre of military wives and children in Kashmir and, 16
    proscription of, 67
    Web-based materials and annual convention, 17
Lashkars
    FATA administration and, 11
LeJ. *See* Lashkar-e-Jhangvi
LeT. *See* Lashkar-e-Taiba
al-Libbi, Abu Farraj
    al-Qaeda membership and, 84 *n*4
    capture of, 1, 14
    FATA and, 14
    work with Farooqui, 22
London Underground attacks
    Jaish-e-Mohammad and Lashkar-e-Taiba and, 18
    militant training in Pakistan and, 2

M

Madaris. See Educational institutions
Maliks
    Federally Administered Tribal Areas and, 10–11
    mullah-*malik* relationship, 13
Marawat, Akhatar Munir
    comments on U.S. assistance, 64
Melmastia
    influx of foreign jihadists and, 12–13
Memon, Tiger
    drug trafficking and, 32–33
Military. *See* Armed forces
Ministry of Interior
    Forward Operating Base project and, 53
    need to reform and revamp police and judicial infrastructure, 45
MMA. *See* Muttahida Majlis-e-Amal
Mohammad, Khaled Sheikh
    al-Qaeda membership and, 84 *n*4
    arrest of, 1, 15, 21
MoI. *See* Ministry of Interior
Mufti, Ja'far Husayn
    Tehrik-e-Nafaz Fiqh-e-Ja'fariyya formation, 25
Musharraf, Pres. Pervez
    assassination attempts against, 2, 14, 17, 21, 22, 48
    "enlightened moderation" and, 17, 22, 68–69
    pledge to end cross-border infiltration of terrorists into Jammu and
        Kashmir, 16, 91 *n*32
    support for the global war on terror, 9
Muttahida Majlis-e-Amal
    education reform efforts and, 23
    Jamaat Islam women's league, 21
    opposition to the global war on terror, 23
    parties in, 95 *n*63
    support for, 23

N

NAB. *See* National Accountability Bureau
NACP. *See* National AIDS Control Program
Naqvi, Ghulum Raza
    SSP founding and, 26
Narcotics. *See* Drugs trafficking

National Accountability Bureau
    armed forces' impact on, 41–42
    powers of, 42, 107 *n*174
    prosecution and investigation figures, 107 *n*175
National AIDS Control Program
    HIV/AIDS prevalence, 32
National Criminal Data Base
    description and funding, 51, 55
    DNA analysis and, 55–56
NCDB. *See* National Criminal Data Base
The 9/11 Commission Report
    recommendation for assistance to Pakistan, 45, 46, 108 *n*9
9/11 terrorist attacks
    Pakistan's stance on international terrorism and, 83 *n*3
Northwest Frontier Province
    drug traffic route through, 29
    FATA administration and, 10
    map, xx
    poppy eradication efforts in, 56
Nuclear arms
    Pakistan as a source for, 79
    security issues, 78–79
    stability of the government and, 4–5, 71, 86 *n*21, 117 *n*31
NWFP. *See* Northwest Frontier Province

O

OEF. *See* Operation Enduring Freedom
Operation Enduring Freedom
    Federally Administered Tribal Areas and, 9–10
    flight of Taliban during, 1
    opium production and, 28, 100 *n*107
Organized crime
    effect on governing legitimacy and effectiveness and, 2–3
    recommendations for programming, 76–77
    success in addressing the threat from, 62

P

Pakhtun
    harboring of militants, 68
    melmastia and, 12–13, 88 *n*13
Pakistan Muslim League

  Islamist organizations and, 23

  Musharraf government and, 96 *n*75, 116 *n*29

  Police Order of 2002 and, 70

Pakistan's People Party

  Islamist organizations and, 23

  Musharraf government and, 96 *n*75, 116 *n*29

  Police Order of 2002 and, 70

Personal Identification Security, Comparison and Evaluation System

  implementation problems, 64

  introduction of, 52

  usefulness of, 61

Pew Research Center

  poll of urban Pakistanis on U.S. foreign policy, 71

Pillai, Leena

  sectarian violence research, 27

PISCES. *See* Personal Identification Security, Comparison and Evaluation
      System

PML. *See* Pakistan Muslim League

Police Order of 2002

  promotion system and, 69, 116 *n*25

  provisions, 45, 69–70, 116 *n*24

Political agents

  responsibilities in FATA, 10–12

  supplementary personnel, 11, 88 *n*9

PPP. *See* Pakistan's People Party

Q

al-Qaeda

  antiterrorist financing programs, 57, 113 *n*72

  arrest of citizens believed to be linked to, 49

  FATA and, 14

  freezing of assets, 57

  links to Sunni sectarian organizations, 62

Qudoos, Ahmed Abdul

  arrest of, 21

S

S/CT. *See* Counterterrorism Office and Bureau of Diplomatic Security,
      Office of Antiterrorism Assistance

Salim, Sheikh Ahmed

  capture of, 15

SCBA. *See* Supreme Court Bar Association
Sectarian violence. *See also* Shi'a group; Sunni group
   aim of, 96 *n*79
   attacks on religious sites, 27
   deaths resulting from Sunni-Shi'a sectarian violence, 2002–2004 (table),
      27
   generalized social instability and, 28
   impact on stability, 27–28
   Iranian revolution of 1979 and, 25–26
   militant sectarian groups, 96 *n*80
   recommendations for programming, 77
   success in addressing the threat from, 62
   Zia's program of Islamicization, 24
Security forces
   assassination attempts against Musharraf and Hayat and, 21–22
   involvement in jihadist terrorism, 21–22
Shaikh, Omar Saeed
   work with Farooqui, 22
Sharif, Nawaz
   Pakistan Muslim League leader, 70
Shi'a group
   deaths resulting from Sunni-Shi'a sectarian violence, 2002–2004 (table),
      27
   Iranian revolution and, 25
   militant training, 98 *n*91
   percentage of the population, 97 *n*83
   Sipah-e-Muhammad Pakistan and, 26
   tax laws and, 24
   Zia's program of Islamicization and, 24
Siddiqui, Shabnam
   sectarian violence research, 27
SIGs. *See* Special Investigative Groups
Singer, Peter
   estimate of the number of *madaris* in Pakistan, 18
Sipah-e-Muhammad Pakistan
   aims of, 26, 97 *n*89
   description, 26
   estimates of followers, 26
   training of members, 26
Sipah-e-Sahaba Pakistan
   goal of, 25
   madaris and, 19

overlapping membership with Jaish-e-Mohammad, 68

overlapping membership with Lashkar-e-Jhangvi, 68

SIUs. *See* Special Investigative Units

SMP. *See* Sipah-e-Muhammad Pakistan

Smuggling. *See* Drugs trafficking; Goods smuggling and human trafficking

Special Investigative Groups

  legislative problems and, 69

  usefulness of, 61

Special Investigative Units

  description and activities, 52, 56

SSP. *See* Sipah-e-Sahaba Pakistan

Stern, Jessica

  estimate of the number of *madaris* in Pakistan, 18

Study focus, 5–6

Study organization and expected benefits, 6–7

Sunni group

  deaths resulting from Sunni-Shi'a sectarian violence, 2002–2004 (table), 27

  Lashkar-e-Jhangvi and, 26

  percentage of the population, 97 *n*83

  religious law interpretation, 24

  Zia's program of Islamicization and, 24

Supreme Court Bar Association

  corruption in the judiciary and, 41

T

Taliban

  FATA support for, 67

  opium ban, 28, 100 *n*106

Tariq, Maulana Azam

  SSP leadership, 25

Tea industry

  smuggling and, 36

Tehrik-e-Nafaz Fiqh-e-Ja'fariyya

  formation of, 25

  promotion and dissemination of pro-Iranian literature, 25

Terrorism. *See* Jihadist terrorism

TI. *See* Transparency International

TI-Bangladesh

  Transparency International–Pakistan and, 113 *n*78

TI-P. *See* Transparency International–Pakistan

TNJF/TJF. *See* Tehrik-e-Nafaz Fiqh-e-Ja'fariyya

Transparency International
    Corruption Perception Index, 2–3, 37–38, 41 105 *n*154
    corruption report, 33
    report on Pakistan, 37
Transparency International–Pakistan
    funding for, 58
    TI-Bangladesh and, 113 *n*78

U

United Nations
    increase in narcotics shipments to Europe and Russia, 29
    study of IV drug abuse, 32
U.S. Agency for International Development
    Democracy and Good Governance program, 57–58
    educational initiatives, 50, 63
    role in assistance to Pakistan, 50
    Transparency International–Pakistan and, 58
U.S. assistance programs. *See also* Assessment of U.S. assistance programs
    amount for FY05, 45, 108 *n*4
    areas of U.S. assistance, 52–58
    border areas and border control, 52–54
    corruption and, 57–59
    corruption and governance, 57–58
    economic support funds, 45
    five-year assistance package, 45, 107 *n*1
    foreign military financing, 45, 70–71, 107n 1
    gaps in coverage, 58
    human trafficking, 56–57
    internal security forces and, 45
    law enforcement capacity and interagency cooperation improvement, 5,
        54–56, 86 *n*22
    narcotics law enforcement, 56
    possible negative impact of assistance, 78
    terrorism financing, 57
    U.S. agencies' strategies and challenges, 46–52
    U.S. Department of Justice, 50–52
    U.S. Department of State, 46–50
U.S. Department of Justice
    Drug Enforcement Agency, 52
    International Criminal Investigative Training Assistance Program, 50–52
U.S. Department of State
    Bureau of International Narcotics and Law Enforcement programs, 46–47

Counterterrorism Office and Bureau of Diplomatic Security, Office of
    Antiterrorism Assistance, 48–50
  estimates of Afghan poppy production, 28, 99 *n*104
  Office to Monitor and Combat Trafficking in Persons, 34–35
  United States Agency for International Development programs, 50
U.S. Trafficking Victims Act
  minimum requirements, 34, 104 *n*140
USAID. *See* U.S. Agency for International Development

W

Waslekar, Sundeep
  sectarian violence research, 27
World Bank
  estimates of goods smuggling, 34
  petroleum product smuggling estimate, 35
  studies of *madaris*, 19, 20

Z

Zia ul-Haqq, Gen. Muhammad
  Islamicization program, 24
Zubaydah, Abu
  al-Qaeda membership and, 84 *n*4
  capture of, 15, 18

About the Authors

C. Christine Fair is a senior research associate within the Center for Conflict Analysis and Prevention at the United States Institute of Peace. Fair specializes in a wide array of South Asian political and military affairs. Prior to joining the Institute in April 2004, she was an associate political scientist at the RAND Corporation. Much of her research has been concerned with security competition between India and Pakistan, Pakistan's internal security, analyses of the causes of terrorism, and U.S. strategic relations with India and Pakistan. She has conducted several analyses for the U.S. government, including an assessment of Indo-U.S. army-to-army relations; an examination of political Islam and its recent developments in Pakistan and Iran; and a comparative study of urban terrorism and state responses in Sri Lanka, Pakistan, and India. Fair collaborates with colleagues at the Naval Postgraduate School, the National Defense University, the National Bureau of Asian Research, and the RAND Corporation. Fair has authored numerous monographs on various aspects of South Asia security as well as chapters within edited volumes on the same. Fair frequently publishes articles in peer-reviewed journals such as the *Study of Conflict and Terrorism, Nationalism and Ethnic Politics, Asian Security,* and *India Review.* Fair is a graduate of the University of Chicago, where she earned a master's degree from the Harris School of Public Policy and a Ph.D. in South Asian Languages and Civilizations.

Peter Chalk is a policy analyst with the RAND Corporation in Santa Monica, California. During the past four years he has worked on projects examining unconventional security threats in Southeast and South Asia; new strategic challenges for the U.S. Air Force in Latin America, Africa, and South Asia; evolving trends in national and international terrorism; Australian defense and foreign policy; international organized crime; the transnational spread of disease; and U.S. military links in the Asia-Pacific. He is a specialist correspondent for *Jane's Intelligence Review* and associate editor of *Studies in Conflict Terrorism.* Chalk has regularly testified before the U.S. Senate on issues pertaining to national and international terrorism and is the author of numerous books, book chapters, monographs, and journal articles dealing with various aspects of low-intensity conflict in the contemporary world. In addition to his RAND position, Chalk serves as an adjunct professor at the Postgraduate Naval School in Monterey, California, and a contractor for the Asia Pacific Center for Security Studies in Honolulu, Hawaii, and the United States Institute for Peace in Washington, D.C. Prior to joining RAND, Chalk was an assistant professor of politics at the University of Queensland, Brisbane, and a postdoctoral fellow in the Strategic and Defense Studies Centre of the Australian National University, Canberra. Apart from his academic posts, Chalk has acted as a research consultant in the United Kingdom, Canada, and Australia and has experience with the UK Armed Forces.

United States Institute of Peace

The United States Institute of Peace is an independent, nonpartisan federal institution created by Congress to promote the prevention, management, and peaceful resolution of international conflicts. Established in 1984, the Institute meets its congressional mandate through an array of programs, including research grants, fellowships, professional training, education programs from high school through graduate school, conferences and workshops, library services, and publications. The Institute's Board of Directors is appointed by the President of the United States and confirmed by the Senate.

Chairman of the Board: J. Robinson West
Vice Chairman: María Otero
President: Richard H. Solomon
Executive Vice President: Patricia Powers Thomson
Vice President: Charles E. Nelson

Board of Directors

J. ROBINSON WEST (Chairman), Chairman, PFC Energy, Washington, D.C.

MARÍA OTERO (Vice Chairman), President, ACCION International, Boston, Mass.

BETTY F. BUMPERS, Founder and former President, Peace Links, Washington, D.C.

HOLLY J. BURKHALTER, Vice President of Government Affairs, International Justice Mission, Washington, D.C.

CHESTER A. CROCKER, James R. Schlesinger Professor of Strategic Studies, School of Foreign Service, Georgetown University

LAURIE S. FULTON, Partner, Williams and Connolly, Washington, D.C.

CHARLES HORNER, Senior Fellow, Hudson Institute, Washington, D.C.

SEYMOUR MARTIN LIPSET, Hazel Professor of Public Policy, George Mason University

MORA L. MCLEAN, President, Africa-America Institute, New York, N.Y.

BARBARA W. SNELLING, former State Senator and former Lieutenant Governor, Shelburne, Vt.

Members ex officio

BARRY F. LOWENKRON, Assistant Secretary of State for Democracy, Human Rights, and Labor

PETER W. RODMAN, Assistant Secretary of Defense for International Security Affairs

RICHARD H. SOLOMON, President, United States Institute of Peace (nonvoting)

FRANCES C. WILSON, Lieutenant General, U.S. Marine Corps; President, National Defense University